words of praise

What to do When Love's in View

As a family man it hurts to see the increasing divorce rate among our people. This book was designed to teach single people how to begin the dating process in a healthy and wise way. If you want to get the girl and keep the girl without compromising your values, then you need to go "cop" this book.

–KIRK FRANKLIN
Gospel Recording Artist

Sticky. Hurtful. Draining. Words like these should never describe a relationship. But the 21st-century's definition of dating has made it so. Thankfully God has sent us Conway and Jada, lifelong friends of mine whose integrity causes the message of this book to speak loud and clear. Prepare to be challenged, convicted, and most importantly compelled to be different as you prepare to embrace the relationships in a way that brings God glory.

–PRISCILLA SHIRER
Bible Teacher and Author

Sincere Christian singles are looking for a refreshing, practical, and godly perspective on relationships. It's time for Christians to establish a healthier norm for relationships to ensure a future with more Christ-centered families. This book is a priceless and proven path to that end. I have found great inspiration and encouragement through the wisdom Conway and Jada offer and it is a wonderful tool for discipling Christian singles.

–LEKESHA R. BARNETT
Assistant Pastor, New Faith Church, Houston, TX

Finally, my friend has put to paper a manual for dating and courting. In 2003, the words in this book were only thoughts that were passionately communicated around a lunch table. If you're single, read it, if you're a married, read it. Men, he calls us to lead and lead we must! Buy this book and read it, repeatedly!

–PASTOR RICK COOPER
Associate Pastor of Married Couples & Single Adults
North Dallas Community Bible Fellowship, Richardson, TX

What to do When Love's in View is truly a thought-provoking and soul-stirring book. This book discusses relationships in a way that is often felt by most people but never, in truth, verbalized by anyone. It is remarkably informative, yet astonishingly realistic; it gives real-life solutions to real-life struggles. Not only should every single person, both male and female, take the time to read this book, but every pastor or counselor-of-singles should read it. After reading the book, you will be equipped with the "antidote" on how to see a clearer picture of Christian "dating" and the roles that God destined for the man and woman.

–ERIC L. ALEXANDER, **Senior Pastor**
St. Luke Baptist Church, North Little Rock, AR

Every now and then, God gives you a friend that you instantly connect with at a deep level. Conway is one of those friends for me. His vulnerability opens the door for honest spiritual exploration, and his insight turns on the light of wisdom so that I can see my heart more clearly. More than anything, though, he helps me see Jesus' heart for me in the midst of my soul-searching. I have no doubt that as you read; he will do the same for you.

–JEFF LAWRENCE, **Equipping Pastor**
Northwest Bible Church, Dallas, TX

Guarding the heart is an ancient principle with modern applications. Conway and Jada take this principle and apply it to the fastest-growing population in America. Every unattached person would do well to ponder these principles and potentially save him or herself a great deal of pain. You should seriously engage the principles of this book before you allow anyone else to engage your heart.

–JAMES R. WOMACK, **Senior Pastor**
Destiny Church, Fort Worth, TX

Helen Keller was asked, "Do you know of anything that's worse than being blind?" She thought for a moment and then said, "Yes, there is one thing worse than being blind—having sight with no vision." Unfortunately my wife and I were once visionless college singles pursuing dating relationships by sight alone. Lacking a vision for singleness proved detrimental in much of our relational decision making as collegians. We needed a guide! It is with great delight that I endorse Dr. Conway and Jada Edwards, _What to do When Love's in View: Finding Focus in Dating and Relationships,_ as a progressive blueprint for guiding singles with real issues to the destination of healthy relationships.

–REV. & MRS. CURTIS WOODS
Kentucky State University, Campus Ministers

What to do When
LOVE's
in VIEW

Finding Focus in Dating and Relationships

Dr. Conway & Jada Edwards

Foreword by Tony Evans

Printed in the United States of America by Aspire Productions

Library of Congress Cataloging-in-Publication Data
Edwards, Conway
        What to do When Love's in View: Finding Focus in Dating and Relationships / Dr. Conway and Jada Edwards

        ISBN
    1.   Dating (Social Customs) 2. Dating (Social Customs)-Religious aspects-Christianity. 3 Man-Woman relationships, 4. Man-Woman relationships-Religious aspects-Christianity 5. Single people – Religious life

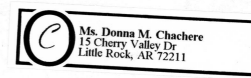

This book is dedicated to our parents,

who modeled the way.

contents

acknowledgements

For Jada and I, many people have shaped our thinking and our values. It takes a village to prepare, develop, and grow children for life as adults. But none are more critical than our parents. Between our parents there is over seventy years of marriage. We want to thank Clyde and Barbara Edwards for their love for God and their commitment to each other. Their faith in God has been inspirational and motivational to us. We also want to thank James and Jean Cobon for their faithfulness to each other and the many sacrifices they have made to give Jada the best opportunity to succeed in life. We love you both.

Pastor Evans, thank you for being our pastor, a model, and a friend. Thank you for the privilege to serve under you in so many areas. Serving as the Director of Singles has been absolutely life-changing! Your commitment to excellence, your priority to family and your love for both of us is really appreciated. Thanks so much for your life and your character.

To our Singles Ministry Management Team at Oak Cliff Bible Fellowship, thank you for the ride of our lives. Working with each of you has been exciting, challenging, and fulfilling. Thank you for the privilege to learn from you and grow with you. Thank you for the memories.

To our Board of Directors for Caribbean Choice for Christ in the United States and the Board of Directors for the National Centre for Christian Leadership Jamaica, thank you for believing in the vision of sharpening influencers to structure institutions that shape individuals with a Christocentric worldview.

We want to thank our family and friends who helped us fine tune this manuscript. To my sister Nicquet, thank you for taking the time to read and edit the book. To Adrienne, Angela, Anitra, Dianne, Mary, Racquel, Sonja, Tim and Ty thank you for your feedback and insight. To the great AR, thank you for the time invested in designing the book.

foreword

Many churches place so much emphasis on marriage and family that many single men and women don't even think about the process or steps that might be necessary to achieve this end result. They also wonder whether or not it is possible to be single and satisfied. Well, I have good news for you. Not only is it possible to be single and live a fulfilled life, but it is sinful to be otherwise. That is, if you are single and unhappy in the role God has given you, you do not yet have a complete handle on God's kingdom view of singleness.

Unfortunately, the church has often helped fuel that sense of incompleteness by its great emphasis on the family. There is nothing wrong with emphasizing the family. But something is wrong with making singles feel like second-class citizens. Pastors often unconsciously fuel the discontent of single believers by helping singles to simply cope with their singleness. But God doesn't simply want single people to cope. He wants them to succeed. Being single should not be a place of stagnation where men and women are in a "holding pattern". Instead, it should be a season of life in which people are still passionately pursuing God's call on their lives while being ready to move in whatever direction He may lead them.

That's why it thrills me that one of my spiritual sons, Conway and his wife Jada, who is like a daughter to me, have now written a guide for developing healthy relationships that prepares singles for lifelong, lasting marriages. For too long we have allowed our culture and the world to influence our lives. Many singles today believe the Bible is silent on issues of dating, relationships, and courting, but God has spoken and Conway and Jada use principles from the Word of God to help those who are unmarried get off the treadmill of unhealthy relationships and pursue responsible, healthy, God-honoring relationships.

This book gives single men and women, regardless of their age, a roadmap to follow in identifying, meeting, courting, and marrying God's best.

Dr. Tony Evans
Senior Pastor, Oak Cliff Bible Fellowship
President, The Urban Alternative

introduction

Jada and I recently purchased a new camera. We called it an "investment" to justify spending a small fortune on something we can't drive, live in, or sit on. In all seriousness, this camera is the professional photographer's dream. It allows for a wide variety of photographic styles and it has all of the capabilities we'll ever need and so much more. One of its features is its ability to switch between manual and automatic focus. We tried using the manual focus when we first purchased it because we wanted to look professional, which I'm sure we did. The problem was that our pictures didn't turn out half as professional as we looked taking them. Since those first attempts, we've decided to rely mainly on the automatic focus. However, we still actually use the manual focus first, to determine the distance we want from our subject and then we engage the auto focus to sharpen the image and determine whether we need a flash. It works splendidly! Our pictures of late have been great and we still get to look a little bit like professionals.

In this book we want to remind you that no matter where you may be in the dating process, or even if you haven't started, God is still the most important "subject" in your life and He deserves your focus. Allow the Holy Spirit within you to be your "auto focus" instead of relying on your own wisdom and strength (manual focus). As you focus on God, you will begin to see His perspective on dating and relationships more clearly. Hopefully, this book will help you to see Him, yourself and your relationships with new eyes.

If you're not convinced that manual focus can get you into trouble, think about these questions. Have you ever been involved in a break-up and asked yourself the standard questions of why the relationship ended? Ever spent a whole day, or an entire month, going over whose fault it was? Have you ever thought that if you'd just done something more, perhaps you could have kept it together? In retrospect, you or the person you were dating probably tried doing things your way (manual focus) instead of including God in your decisions regarding the relationship.

By looking at the statistics, it's clear that most of us tend to favor doing things our way; this approach has proven unsuccessful. In fact, it seems that our society as a whole is doing something wrong in this area of dating relationships. Let's take a look at what statistics reveal about first marriages. Based on 2000 census data, the Centers for Disease Control and Prevention reported that 20% of first marriages end within 5 years, 33% end within 10 years, and 50% end within

20 years. For those in their second marriages the statistics were worse. Approximately 54% of second marriages end within 5 years, 75% end within 10 years, and 83% end within 15 years. Overall, about 60% of all marriages eventually end in divorce.

> **Overall, about 60% of all marriages eventually end in divorce.**

For all these numbers to be meaningful you need to open your eyes and look beyond the black-and-white data from the latest studies. What these numbers represent are shattered dreams, crushed hopes, and devastated hearts. Most people concede that these numbers are staggering statistics of failure, but not many seem to have solutions for this growing crisis. So let me ask you. How can we get this right? For the sake of our lives, our destinies in Christ, the ministries that God has entrusted to us, and the next generation coming after us, we must get this right.

Marital problems often stem from issues that initially arise from dating relationships. Problems in dating relationships are often rooted in unresolved issues within ourselves. So if we are to start anywhere, we must begin with ourselves. We must first look at who God wants us to be as individuals and gauge how we're progressing before we can deal with the wider world of dating and relationships. As Christians, we sometimes react as though God has not spoken on the subject of dating, but nothing could be further from the truth. God's Word provides clear insight and fundamental principles that help us approach relationships from a biblical perspective.

Now, I'll be the first to admit that I've not always applied these fundamental truths to my own life. The truth is this book was birthed from a search I embarked on after a painful experience (see chapter one). I thank God for that season of my life; this search changed my life forever. In these next few pages I'll share with you what I discovered along this painful, powerful, and above all, valuable journey.

As you read this book, I hope you will embark on a personal journey of your own and elevate who you are becoming. That "elevation" begins with comprehending the fundamental roles of men and women. For too long we have misunderstood the core meaning of manhood and womanhood and the devastating effects on our society are painfully evident. Yet Jesus said, "you will know the truth, and the truth will set you free" (John 8:32). It is my prayer that this book will help you see the truth of God's Word about important principles for engaging in healthy relationships.

the journey begins

1

he year was 1994, and I had been in America for about three years. I was pursuing my master's degree in business while serving as youth pastor for a church in San Diego, California. As far as I was concerned, life was wonderful. I was enjoying school, but most of all, I was enjoying my role as a youth pastor. Little did I know—my life was about to change. One day, while studying, a young lady ran up to me, crying.

"You don't know me," she began, "but I know you. You're the youth pastor at our church. I just lost my thesis when the computer crashed. Could you pray for me?"

"I'd love to, let's pray," I replied. After all, I thought, I was a youth pastor at the church and it was my duty to support any member during such an anxious time. That prayer began an interesting relationship between us. We started talking more at church and we began spending time together outside of church. In no time at all, we became very good friends. She was a sweet young lady who loved ministry. We had great conversations. We laughed together, ministered together, went out on dates, and took trips together. She became an integral part of my life. I enjoyed her personality and her company; it was great being around a young lady who genuinely loved God. Because she was a servant by nature, she often helped me finish papers for school. If I needed her to run an errand, she would do it. She would bring me food or cook for me if she thought I was hungry, and she would even do my laundry without me asking. Whatever I needed, her primary goal became to satisfy and serve *me*. I was clearly the primary benefactor in our relationship. For a while, I considered whether she was the one for me, but I couldn't make up my mind. I was undecided and scared and did not want to make a mistake. Quite honestly, our friendship was great and very comfortable, so I never felt any urgency to make a decision. Deep down, it felt good to be around someone who really cared and had so much affection for me. I also knew she respected me as a leader in ministry, but I was too young, too selfish, and too prideful to even consider that her emotional investment was far greater than mine.

> *Deep down, it felt good to be around someone who really cared and had so much affection for me.*

A year and a half later, after consulting with mentors and spending a lot of time in prayer, I felt the call of God to attend seminary in Texas. A couple of friends, this young lady included, flew with me to Dallas to help me get settled. When they were leaving and heading back to California, I pulled her aside and began to talk with her. I knew that if I was struggling with the direction of the relationship when we were in the same city, there was no way we would be able

6

to maintain our relationship while we were apart. I decided that it would be best for both of us if we just went ahead and ended the relationship.

"I don't think we can do this long-distance thing anymore," I said.

She responded, "What do you mean? I thought it was just a matter of time before we got married. We've spent so much time together and we've gotten to know each other so well." I could see the hurt in her eyes and hear it in her voice. But I continued.

"No," I replied, "I just think that God is calling me in another direction, so I'm just going to go." I tried my best to be sensitive and even justified my decision with God's leading. Surely she could understand.

After what seemed like an eternity of awkward silence, she spoke. This young lady, whom I had known to be so gentle, tender, and caring, spoke a very bold statement to me. She looked me square in the eyes and said, "God's got great plans for you, but if you don't fix this issue, it's going to derail you." I couldn't believe what I was hearing. Instead of being overtaken by emotion, she was calling me out! She was basically saying that how I was choosing to deal with our relationship was a warning sign. If I didn't learn how to relate to women in a healthy way, I was going to run into big problems for the rest of my life. I appreciated her concern but I didn't think much of it.

I thought that was the end of it, but several months after she left

Dallas I received a phone call from her.

"Conway, I care about you too much to leave this problem unchecked." I didn't know where she was going with this but I decided to hear her out.

"Alright, then let's talk about this."

"No, I don't think you'll listen to me if we talked one-on-one about this issue." Again, I didn't know where her thinking was but I could not have imagined what came next.

About a week later I got a call from one of the elders at my former church. "Conway, I can't believe what I'm hearing about you from this young lady. We want to fly you back to San Diego and hear your side of the story." I was absolutely shocked, and thought to myself, had she gotten the elders of my church involved? Was it that serious? I mean, I knew I could have handled it better but this seemed a bit extreme. I couldn't believe they were going to fly me from Texas to California just to have a conversation about a relationship.

I decided to consult some counselors from school and the church I was currently attending and asked them if they thought I needed to go back to meet with my former elders. Of the ten people I consulted, nine said the San Diego church was no longer my authority. Therefore I was under no obligation to go back.

But one person said, "You need to return." The Holy Spirit used that one person to convict me. I knew I had to go back even though

I was not looking forward to it.

My former elders paid the plane fare, flew me back, and seemingly in a matter of seconds, I found myself in a room with ten elders from my church in San Diego. The worship leader, who had been a spiritual mentor for me, and the young lady and her best friend were also in attendance that day. I still wasn't quite sure about what was to transpire, but it was suddenly clear that my charm and charisma weren't going to help me in this situation. I felt like I was about to be interrogated by a congressional committee.

The elders started by asking her to share her story. Over the next hour and fifteen minutes, she shared everything that had taken place in our relationship. Every interaction, every conversation, and every act of service came to the light. Hearing her perspective was startling. She remembered everything in grave detail—almost every date, every trip we had taken; it had all been etched in her memory. Although I had never had sex with this young woman, I had gone as far as I could go. I pushed the envelope regarding physical intimacy. As she spoke, she shared her heart and deep hurt. By the end of her story there was not a dry eye in the room, including mine. I was blown away as I listened to her talk about our interactions. She bared her soul and talked about how she had expected and anticipated marriage based on the nature of our relationship and my actions. She told everyone in that room how she had trusted and looked up to me as a boyfriend and a ministry leader and then she told us all how I had shattered her heart.

With Kleenex being passed around the room and everybody

drying their tears, I was asked if I had anything to say.

> *How does a man, who's truly in love with God, handle this gift called "woman" in such a way that protects her heart and doesn't hurt her in the dating process?*

"No. Everything she said was true." I managed.

In a word, it was devastating. I had never before understood my behavior as so irresponsible and I definitely didn't anticipate how it could impact a woman's heart. The potential impact of what one man's casual actions can do to a woman's heart is astonishing. I had never realized how different the emotions of women are from those of men or how easily they trusted us. The weight of what it meant to be a responsible man who loves God came crashing down on me.

Those elders—some of the most godly men I know to this day—said, "Conway, here's what we need you to do. We'll pay for Christian counseling for you, but we need you to understand that you are responsible for your actions when you approach one of God's precious jewels. We don't want this to happen to another woman again, not at your expense and not by your doing. Here's a calling card. Anytime you need to talk, you call us at our expense because we care for you and we want to prepare you for what God has in store for you."

I left that room, my mind heavy with questions for which I had no answers. How in the world was I supposed to get this right? I cared about this young lady and had never meant to hurt her - but I did. I wanted us to be able to enjoy a special friendship without the pressure of commitment - but we couldn't.

How does a man, who's truly in love with God, handle this gift called "woman" in such a way that protects her heart and doesn't hurt her in the dating process? Can a man and woman truly just be friends? What are the things that a man does to encourage a woman's emotions?

This experience was the springboard to an extensive personal journey that God was about to take me on so that I could learn these answers and share them with every unmarried person I knew. I couldn't even imagine how many men had no clue how their casual behaviors impacted women. Over the remaining chapters of this book I will share with you the principles God brought to light during my journey. He showed me how important it is to know myself, know who I am becoming, and how a godly man should interact with women in a healthy way.

the man you are becoming

2

I really enjoy seeing good leadership in action. It was game six of the NBA 2006 finals. The Dallas Mavericks won the first two games in Dallas and everyone thought the series would be a sweep. The Miami Heat, however, rallied to win the next three games at home and led the basketball series three games to two, with the last two games to be played in Dallas. Most sportscasters still favored Dallas to come back and win the championship, but Pat Riley would have none of it.

Pat Riley, coach of the Miami Heat, told his team that he packed one suit, one shirt, and one tie. There were two games left but if Miami won game six, the series would be over and the title would be theirs. Pat saw the victory, created the vision and the environment so that his team could see it and believe it as well, and he laid out a strategy to get the team to their destination. That's leadership!

Just as Pat Riley led his team with vision, strategy, and a model, God is asking us as men to have a vision for our lives and our relationships, a strategy that will lead us to our destination and a willingness to model Christ along the way.

For Pat Riley, that was a one-time event, but God is calling you and me to consistently lead with vision through life with all of its ups and downs.

So what does it take to lead in a godly manner? What does it mean to be a godly man? Since the essence of manhood is to initiate and to lead, you must ask if you are on the way to becoming a leader, and a godly man? These were the questions I had to ask myself after what happened in San Diego. In order to understand how not to make that mistake again, I needed some answers.

God created man with an innate sense to make the first move, to start, and to lead, which implies that a man must be headed in some particular direction. 1 Corinthians 11:3 states that God created man to lead; "But I want you to know that Christ is the head of every man, and the man is the head of a woman, and God is the head of Christ."

Just as Christ made the first move and initiated (led) a relationship with mankind, so it is that man must take the initiative and lead. I know that the word "lead" can be thought of negatively, especially to today's modern woman. Women today are more in control of their education, careers, and well-being than ever before and the whole idea of being "led" makes them a little skeptical. This skepticism is supported when, after a cursory glance, they realize some men don't know why they exist or what journey they are on let alone how to take someone with them. But men, if we will step up and really seek to understand who God has called us to be, we can begin to rewrite the many sad stories of failed dating relationships and failed marriages.

In Ephesians 5:25, the Word of God commands husbands to love their wives like Christ loved the church. Christ loved relentlessly. He initiated His love in the midst of rejection (Rom. 5:8). As a single man, how are you preparing yourself to love like this? How will you learn to initiate and lead regardless of potential rejection? What's the first step in doing this? The first thing we must do to redefine ourselves is to become R.E.A.L. men.

Do you want to know what makes a R.E.A.L. man? Here's my take on the idea of being a R.E.A.L. man, a concept Robert Lewis introduces in _Raising a Modern Day Knight_.

Reject Passivity

First of all, a R.E.A.L. man has vision. If you're a R.E.A.L man, then you know where you are going. In order to know where you're going and move toward that vision, men must reject passivity. In Genesis 2:15 we read, "The Lord God took the man and placed him in the orchard in Eden to care for and maintain it." Laziness (passivity) is not implied anywhere in this passage because God expects for men to be active, dynamic, and energetic reflections of Himself. Just like a farmer has to know what vegetable or fruit he wants to grow, then sow the necessary seeds, and tend the crop to produce those fruits or vegetables, so a man should know where God wants him to go and take the necessary steps to get there. That includes sowing good habits and cultivating and tending the garden (job, home, body, and resources) God gives him.

Every man must possess a clear picture of what a healthy, godly man looks like. One of the most devastating realities in our culture today is that for a variety of reasons many men do not have a clear picture of manhood. In other words, they don't know who they are trying to become. Notice I said *who* they are trying to become, not *what*. Wanting to become a great businessman, an athlete, or a husband still doesn't say *who* you want to be. It simply defines *what* you want to be.

> One of the most devastating realities in our culture today is that for a variety of reasons many men do not have a clear picture of manhood.

Becoming a healthy man requires you to have a vision for your life which means you must be actively pursuing the call of God in your heart. Rejecting passivity means we don't just wait for life to happen; we make life happen! We can't allow ourselves to just blend into the scenery. Men, we weren't made to just exist; we were made to contribute! How will your life make a difference?

Eternity

Secondly, a R.E.A.L. man lives for the world that is to come, not for this world. In other words, a R.E.A.L. man lives his life in light of <u>eternity</u>. Ecclesiastes 3:10-11 states, "I have seen the business that God has given to the sons of men to be busy with. He has made everything beautiful in its time; also he has put eternity into man's mind, yet so that he cannot find out what God has done from the beginning to the end."

All of humanity forever will be restless. The question one must ask is, why? A man can never be content with simple existence; he must always look deeper for purpose and meaning. According to verse 11 in the above passage, God has placed "*eternity* into man's mind." This simply means that no experience in this life on earth—no matter how varied, stimulating or memorable—can provide true contentment because we have a restless longing for something eternal. This longing is tied to God's vision of having an eternal perspective (2 Corinth. 4:18), therefore true contentment can only be found in God. As men, we have a responsibility to recognize the brevity of life and be good stewards here on earth. Living with eternity in our minds means that we live our lives to make God look good (bring Him glory) until He takes us home to heaven. We must live for what is to come as opposed to simply living for today.

International students who come to the United States for education are a great example of living for what is to come. When they come to the States, everything they do and buy has to be examined through the eyes of their future plans for returning home. If they are going to buy a car, get married, or make any major decisions, they have to consider how it will fit into their culture and their future goals. They have to be careful of major purchases that they make because they won't be taking much with them when they return to their home country. They have to travel light and be willing to live

17

in such a way that anyone who encounters them realizes where their focus lies.

What is true of international students going to school in the United States should be true of all men. Just as these students are away from home to accomplish a task, so too is every man of God. We are here on earth to accomplish His plan for our lives, a plan He has put in our hearts. As men, we cannot be so consumed with the accumulation of "things" and becoming successful according to the world's standards that we lose focus of the real reason we're here. In other words, don't pick up temporary things you can't carry back to your eternal home (heaven). If we can't embrace this mindset for ourselves, it won't be something we can teach our families.

Aware

The third characteristic of a R.E.A.L. man is awareness. We must be <u>aware</u> of who we are, how we think, and how our heritage, life experiences, skills, gifts, and personal temperaments will impact us as we interact with women in relationships. Paul wrote that if anyone had the right to brag about his or her earthly status it was he. He was "circumcised on the eighth day, from the people of Israel and the tribe of Benjamin, a Hebrew of Hebrews. I lived according to the law as a Pharisee" (Phil. 3:5-6). Paul had an elite birthright and lived a high-class life before becoming a Christian. Why did he take the time to say all this? This was a lead up to verse 7, where he declared, "But these assets I have come to regard as liabilities because of Christ." Paul demonstrates self-awareness in this passage. He knew himself well enough to know exactly what he was giving up to follow Christ.

He also knew his high earthly status could be a stumbling block in his ministry if he did not constantly "count it as worthless or regard it as a liability." Along with being made ruler over what God gives us and living today in light of heaven, we must be prepared to take ownership of our behavior and our actions, especially in the area of relationships when we are considering marriage.

This also includes a man's responsibility for the "baggage" he will bring to a relationship. I can't emphasize enough how important it is to know yourself. The experience I shared in chapter one opened the door to an internal search. That young lady and my elders saw a serious flaw in my character, and if I wanted to grow as a man I had to dig deeper. Of course that situation was just the start of a long thread beginning to unravel as I discovered the experiences, family background, cultural and spiritual values, and personal beliefs governing my behavior. It is just as important for us to know our strengths and gifts but we usually don't have a problem identifying them. As men, our God-given responsibilities include leading courageously, connecting emotionally, loving selflessly, discipling comprehensively, and fighting faithfully against the subtle influences of the world. We are obligated to try and understand the many facets of ourselves that may hinder us or help us in successfully fulfilling those responsibilities.

Ephesians 5:23 reads, "…because the husband is the head of the wife as also Christ is the head of the church—He himself being the Savior of the body." Men, we cannot be the head of anything or anyone without first being prepared to accept the consequent responsibility. Are you ready to lead? Are you ready to be the head of your household? Are you ready to disciple a family?

Love

Are you prepared to <u>love</u> consistently? This is the final quality of a
R.E.A.L. man. Paul admonished us, "Husbands, love your wives just
as Christ loved the church and gave himself for her" (Eph. 5:25). One
of the greatest qualities about Christ's love for us is its consistency—it
never changes. As a result, love means you are willing and prepared to
give all of yourself for the wife with whom God has blessed you. This
means loving your potential wife regardless of her actions. Loving her
on the good days and on the bad days, on the days when it comes
naturally and easily, and on the days when it's a struggle and demands
a concerted effort. Having Christ as our model, we must be willing
to love her until death. Just as we can have confidence in Christ's
unchanging and unconditional love for us, your potential mate
should have confidence to believe that you will love her regardless of
her behavior, her moods, and her decisions. We must learn to love
consistently, comprehensively, and completely.

In summary, R.E.A.L men <u>reject passivity</u>, realize that they
must keep <u>eternity</u> in mind, are <u>aware</u> of both their strengths and
weaknesses, and <u>love</u> consistently. Men, we must be R.E.A.L in all of
our relationships, not just with potential mates. Being R.E.A.L. must
be a part of our character. If we can't exhibit these qualities with our
family, friends, those in authority over us, and co-workers, we have
a slim chance that they will magically appear when we're ready to
pursue a woman. Before we can even take the step of praying for God
to send us a wife, we must be honest, transparent, and R.E.A.L. with

ourselves and with God who created us.

Earlier I highlighted four important attributes of a godly man. Now let's talk about how men should interact with women in a healthy way. How can we put action to those attributes? The following are six behaviors from God's Word which will help us better understand what it means to be a godly man in the area of relationships.

1. *A godly man does not engage in emotionally based relationships with women to whom he has not made a commitment (i.e., marriage, family, etc.).*

If you have a relationship that you use to meet your emotional and/or physical needs as they arise or a female "friend" that subs as a girlfriend whenever you feel like it – you're probably in or headed toward an emotionally based relationship. These are non-family relationships where you play the role of protector, comforter, counselor, or provider, and where either of you would be hurt (even if you wouldn't admit it) if the other entered a similar relationship with someone else. If you cannot see yourself married to a woman with whom you have an emotionally based relationship, then here is the question you must ask yourself—*Is this behavior appropriate for a godly man?*

Genesis 2:24 states, "That is why a man leaves his father and mother and unites with his wife, and they become a new family." This Scripture underscores the importance of commitment when a man and woman make the decision to come together. Commitment means permanence.

2. *A godly man chooses not to lust after a woman (to satisfy himself at her expense).* We are exhorted in 2 Timothy 2:22 to "… keep away from youthful passions (lusts), and pursue righteousness, faithfulness, love, and peace, in company with others who call on the Lord from a pure heart." This is a decision like the one Joseph made when he fled the house of Potiphar in Genesis 39 after Potiphar's wife propositioned him. It's a *choice*, brothers, and you must make the right choice each time. James wraps it up nicely in James 1:15 when he writes, "But each one is tempted when he is lured and enticed by his own desires. Then when desire conceives, it gives birth to sin, and when sin is full grown, it gives birth to death." This means we must try our best to avoid situations that may "conceive" desires (lust) in our hearts. It also means when we find ourselves with lust in our hearts we ought to do everything using God's power within us not to act on it. Look guys, let's be practical. Sometimes we have to go the extra mile to not take the second look or to make sure our eyes stay on her eyes during conversation. I have some personal boundaries that I maintain, such as not being one-on-one with a woman unless it's absolutely necessary. If it is, I make sure someone else knows

where we are and what we're doing and how long it should take. The point is, being visual in nature isn't an excuse for letting lust take up room in our hearts. God knows how he made us and He still has a standard of purity for us.

3. *A godly man understands God's design for sex.* We read in 1 Corinthians 6:18, "Flee sexual immorality! Every sin a person commits is outside of the body. But he who sins sexually sins against his own body." Sexual sin involves sinning against one's *own body.* Sex is specifically designed for marriage and sex outside of marriage can prove detrimental to both the man and the woman. You may think this command is a "given," but you would be surprised how often sex outside of marriage is an issue single Christian men struggle with. Some men are so consumed with their personal struggle they begin to debate the absoluteness of God's Word on the subject. If you're a man who has engaged in this debate, let's be clear. Sexual purity outside of marriage is not an option! There is no room for interpretation. It is a sin to find sexual fulfillment anywhere else but with your wife. This includes masturbation, various forms of pornography, and any other methods the world or our flesh may invent. As a godly man, you would be wise to remember 1 Corinthians 6:19 "Or do you not know that your body is the temple of the Holy Spirit who is in you, whom you have from God, and you are not your own? For you were bought at a price. Therefore glorify God with your body."

4. *A godly man knows that inappropriate interactions with women can have a lasting negative effect on their view of men and his view of*

women. Yes, God is concerned about our day-to-day interactions with women. Therefore we should desire to treat them and speak to them in a way that honors God. Paul charges Timothy to "speak to younger men as brothers, older women as mothers, and younger women as sisters—with complete purity" (1 Tim.5:1-2). This is a choice you have to make. Paul reminds us of it in Ephesians 4:21-24 when he writes, "If indeed you heard about him and were taught in him, just as the truth is in Jesus. You were taught with reference to your former way of life to lay aside the old man who is being corrupted in accordance with deceitful desires, to be renewed in the spirit of your mind, and to put on the new man who has been created in God's image—in righteousness and holiness that comes from truth." Paul is basically saying to ditch whatever old habits and tendencies you had which leads to immorality and embrace new habits of holiness.

Men, now is the time to put off the former conduct. It's time we move from *players* to *protectors.* There is a fine line between being considerate or complimentary and being flirtatious or fishing for compliments. There is a fine line between being a gentleman and treating her like a girlfriend. These lines can be hard to see, but trust me; they exist clearly in a woman's mind. When in doubt go to the men who hold you accountable or the men who give you counsel. You can even ask your mother, sister, or any female relative. They are usually more than willing to help you draw the line!

5. *A godly man views himself as a leader in any relationship and takes a lead role, accordingly, in the establishment of a godly household.*

Joshua 24:15 makes the bold declaration, "... choose today whom you will worship...But I and my family will worship the Lord!" Here is yet another reminder of how important it is for us to reject passivity. As men, we set the tone for our homes and our families. This is a role you begin to embrace <u>only</u> when you are pursuing a woman for marriage. Herein lies one of the many problems with casual dating. How can you take the lead in a relationship you're not committed to?

6. *A godly man uses God's Word as the ultimate guide for his life.* David declares in Psalm 119:105, "Your instructions are a lamp that shows me where to walk, and a light that shines on my path." In fact, this entire psalm is dedicated to the importance of God's Word and His commandments. Today we have so many books on manhood that we don't know which way to turn. As men, we sometimes receive mixed messages from preachers too. Who's right? The only way to discern or understand what truth we need to cling to is to be led by the light of God's Word. Even advice from the best pastor, our closest friend, the wisest counselor, or this book must be tried and tested by God's unwavering standard. God speaks to us as men through His Word. He gives us guidance and discernment and refreshes us as leaders. Whether or not we realize it, the amount of time we spend in His Word is evident in how we live our lives.

As we embark on this journey of finding out who God wants us to be and how He wants us to live, it is our duty to seriously commit our lives, bodies, thoughts, dreams, and relationships to Christ. If you can grasp the magnitude of who God designed you to be, you can begin to see all of life—including relationships—through His eyes.

I can only imagine all of the thoughts swirling through your mind right now. Maybe a personal story can help or at least remind you that you're not alone. On the following pages, one of my mentees shares what he experienced the first time he heard this message.

one man's experience

My initial experience with hearing Pastor Conway teach this message of "Engaging the Heart" was with a group of men who all had a desire to know what it meant to engage the heart of a woman. I must admit that my expectations were pretty low for what I would receive from the session. I expected the time to be a social hour where this group of men created more questions than answers, added some spiritual content, and ultimately came away with very little if anything.

Instead, within a short period of time I received new revelation that I still carry with me. My heart was longing for the answers that my mind could not exactly comprehend and I knew the truth the minute I heard it. Many of the men in the session that day, whose ages ranged from 18 to over 40, began to reflect on past relationships and in that moment, for the first time, it all made sense. We had all engaged and captured the hearts of women we had known and were clueless to that fact, for the most part.

It was so simple, yet it had eluded me for years. Who

would have ever believed that something as simple as my conversation could engage a woman's heart? In my mind I was just being friendly with the hope of developing a friendship but nothing more— well maybe a little more but the rest of the commitment was years off. I realized that through my conversation or considerate actions, I could speak to the hearts of women with much deeper meaning than I could understand on my own. This revelation has changed me forever.

After I left the session, I no longer understood how to behave or react toward women. My reality had been shaken up and I realized that things were a lot more serious than I first perceived. I now had a responsibility to guard the hearts of women and treat them as my sisters. Part of that responsibility meant that I would have to be on alert when interacting with women.

I now understand, in a practical way, that if a woman is not your wife or engaged to be your wife, then she is your sister and should be treated as such in all purity. I can no longer straddle the fence between friend and love interest. So until the time when God presents her to me, I do the work that God has given me to serve Him. I work in preparation of what is to come and to minimize distractions from fulfilling His will.

the woman you are becoming

A s a woman, I (Jada) have discovered that the answers to many of life's questions can be answered in one place. You guessed it -the mall! One day I found myself in need of a particular item and I knew the nearby mall would have what I needed. I arrived and found myself standing in the middle of once-familiar territory feeling quite disoriented. The mall had recently undergone an extensive expansion. It had more than doubled in size and the number of stores seemed countless. I was there to run a quick errand. I knew what I needed to purchase and I knew that it was in the mall somewhere, but I didn't know which store would have it or where that store might be.

I took a chance and started walking in the direction that looked right. I was really lost and I only hoped I was getting closer to my destination and not walking farther away with each step. After passing a few stores, I saw the light. No, it wasn't the store I was looking for. It was better. I had found the mall directory! And of course the first thing I looked for was the little triangle that declares "You Are Here." Once I realized where I was in relation to my destination, my perspective and methods changed. First, I studied the directory to locate the closest store that would have what I needed. Then I noted some key landmarks I would need to pass by to get to that store and then I was off, feeling confident and walking a lot faster than before.

> *Before you can begin to chart a course for a specific destination, you must know where you're starting.*

My experience at the mall is similar to our experiences as women. We have destinations that we are trying to reach that may be related to family, career, school, fitness, or spiritual growth. Of course, many women have one destination that consumes them more than any other, and that is marriage. The problem is that we find ourselves as lost as I was trying to navigate through that mall. We know what we need in general and we know that only God has it, but we don't know what that looks like in our everyday lives or which direction to go in order to pursue it.

Before you can begin to chart a course for a specific destination, you must know where you're starting. So often we take the approach I initially took. We decide to "take our chances" and we start moving in a direction hoping and praying that we will wind up in the right place. If you walk the mall long enough, there is always a chance that you'll find the store and items you were looking for. However, striving to be a godly woman doesn't work that way. You can wander for a very long time and still miss the mark. To mature into the woman God has designed you to be, you must first know the woman you are today. One of the big issues in marriages today is that people don't realize how much of who they are and how they think shape how they relate to their spouses. Only after you take assessment of where you are in relation to your own baggage, issues, life experiences, and natural personality, can you begin to think about preparing for a relationship, courtship, or marriage.

In the following paragraphs I will outline some foundational biblical characteristics that are critical to fulfilling your role as a woman of God. As you read through them, consider where you are in each area. Which area is a particular struggle? In which areas do you naturally flourish?

In the beginning, God created the woman to be a helpmate. In essence, He created us to S.E.R.V.E. If that word "serve" makes you cringe—and for many women it will—let me just ask that you stop right now and pray for God to open your mind and make your heart fertile soil for what He has to say.

Ready? Good. Now, let's move on.

Support

Woman was originally designed to <u>support</u> and undergird a man who understands his purpose and recognizes his destiny. Genesis 2:18 says, "The Lord God said, 'It is not good for the man to be alone. I will make a companion for him who corresponds to him' ". Her role is not a weak one. On the contrary, it is one of strength and perseverance but it is frequently misconstrued as "less than" or "second class". In reality, it simply defines position not value. However, it does imply that a woman is following a man who needs her help. If a man needs her help, he must be doing something that he alone can't do. All this leads us to conclude that a man must have a vision, task, or calling that requires a suitable helpmate to support him. If a man is *not* doing something so big that he needs our help, we tend to get restless; and when we get restless, we often try to take control.

Empower

Second, a woman is called to <u>empower</u>, nurture, and develop those around her. Proverbs 31:12 says, "She brings him good and not evil all the days of her life," and verse 23 states, "Her husband is well-known in the city gate when he sits with the elders of the land." These verses speak about how a woman gives strength to her husband so much so that he gains a widespread reputation. Please note that to empower does not mean to control. While controlling exerts power, empowerment gives power. In order for us to be empowerers, we have to give up our desire for credit and recognition.

Relate

We have also been uniquely gifted to <u>relate</u> and connect with others, especially our families. This is the third attribute of a woman who S.E.R.V.E.s. In Proverbs 31: 26-28 we read, "She opens her mouth with wisdom, and loving instruction is on her tongue. She watches over the ways of her household, and does not eat the bread of idleness. Her children rise up and call her blessed, her husband also praises her." Not only does this woman relate well to others with wisdom and kindness, she also relates well to her family and they praise her for it. It is interesting to note that the praises come *after* the verse dealing with her tongue (v. 26). There must be a connection there. Controlling the tongue is particularly critical for us as women. Our sharp tongues have been the cause of many broken relationships and hurt feelings. Depending on how we use it, the tongue can hinder or help us in relating and connecting to others.

Value a Covering

The fourth characteristic of a woman who S.E.R.V.E.s is that she <u>values</u> the covering in her life. As we have mentioned before (Chapter 2), Genesis 2:24 talks about a man leaving his mother and father and uniting with his wife. This principle applies to both men and women. It doesn't necessarily mean that you can't leave your parents' house until you get married. It does mean that as long as you are not married you shouldn't "leave" the authority of your mother and/or father. This is because we must <u>always</u> be under a covering. God never planned on us living life without a spiritual authority to guide us. As women, we should have a spiritual protector that serves as our covering until we are married. This passage does not indicate a limit on the age of the woman—only that she must be unmarried. As a woman, you don't outgrow the need for a spiritual covering, and your covering doesn't necessarily have to be older than you or even be related to you.

Having said that, let me still encourage you to use wisdom in choosing a spiritual father. If he is not a relative, it is best that he is married and his wife is someone with whom you have a genuine relationship. The main function of a spiritual father, or spiritual parents, is to provide general godly wisdom as issues in life arise. This is so you have a sounding board to bring balance to your decisions and choices. A few years ago a widow, who was about 60 years old, decided to remarry. Before she committed to marrying her new love, she made sure that her son and one of her nephews talked with him and assessed his character. She valued them as her spiritual covering. No matter your age, any relationship you are in needs to come under the authority in your life. The problem is that many women have no authority to "leave" and often find that they "unite" with anyone that comes along. I urge you to value your need for a spiritual covering. If you don't have one, or don't know of any potential candidates, earnestly ask God to provide a covering for you. **One last caution: beware of a man who doesn't respect the spiritual father or parents in your life. This may clue you in as to how he views authority.**

Enhance

Lastly, a woman who S.E.R.V.E.s <u>enhances</u> and impacts the lives of the people around her. Proverbs 31: 11-15 says, "The heart of her husband has confidence, in her, and he has no lack of gain. She brings him good and not evil all the days of her life. She obtains wool and flax, and she is pleased to work with her hands. She is like the merchant ships; she brings her food from afar. She also gets up while it is still night, and provides food for her household and a portion to her female servants."

Everyone around her is better because she is in the house. Sometimes our tendency is to focus on enhancing external things. We want to look nice, have a nice home, and have nice-looking children and these are important. However, as women, the most important thing we can enhance is our hearts. When we beautify our spirits, we impact the lives of everyone around us. As we grow and develop, everyone around us grows and develops as well. Whom are you developing? Who is becoming a better person because of your presence?

Simply put, being called to S.E.R.V.E. means that we prioritize others over ourselves. Think about the women whom you admire. Mothers, grandmothers, aunts, and sisters are all givers. They consistently prioritized the needs of their families and friends, and that is why they have impacted us and influenced us so deeply. You may be thinking of how much you love the women in your life and wondering how in the world you'll ever be like that. We are more concerned with "being taken advantage of" and we often convince ourselves that we can't S.E.R.V.E. others the way our matriarch's did. But Jesus clearly prioritized servants when He told the disciples in Matthew 23:11, "the greatest among you will be your servant." He valued and modeled the principle of servanthood. In God's eyes the grace to serve is an act of humility and one of the greatest virtues. Jesus' words in Matthew 23:12 echo this: "And whoever exalts himself will be humbled, and whoever humbles himself will be exalted." So it follows, as women pursuing God's plan for our lives, we should **S**upport, **E**mpower, **R**elate, **V**alue, and **E**nhance, and this attitude should be consistent in all of our relationships. Are you supportive of your co-workers, your girlfriends, your family members? Do you empower others, or do you have to be in control? Do you respect all of the authority figures God has placed in your life (father, pastor, boss, etc.)? How do you measure up as a woman who is called to S.E.R.V.E?

Once you understand who you are and where you are in your pursuit of godliness, you can embrace the S.E.R.V.E. concept and evaluate yourself in each of those areas. In other words, once you fully understand and accept the primary functions of a woman, you can then find specific principles that you can practice on a daily basis. Remember, these are principles and they are not to be interpreted in a restricted or legalistic sense. The point is not to create more *rules* to follow but to see the fruit that is produced from a *relationship* with Christ as we strive to be like Him.

> *The point is not to create more rules to follow but to see the fruit that is produced from a relationship...*

The following are eight behaviors from God's Word that we believe model the actions of a godly woman specifically in the area of relationships. My goal is to provide you with a guide in which to evaluate yourself and your relationship.

1. *A godly woman understands that it is inappropriate to pursue or engage in physical, emotional, or spiritual oneness with a man she is not married to.* The apostle Paul writes in Ephesians 5:3-4, "But among you there must not be either sexual immorality, impurity of any kind, or greed, as these are not fitting for the saints. Neither should there be vulgar speech, foolish talk, or coarse jesting—all of which are out of character—but rather thanksgiving." Paul says

it's more than just abstaining from sex; it's about watching what you say and how you behave. For many women, our struggle isn't physical; it's spiritual and emotional. It's those men "friends" that you have to be careful about. Be careful about praying with or sharing other spiritually and emotionally intimate experiences one-on-one with men. For example, weddings and funerals are significant emotional events so we cannot casually invite a man to share that with us. We have to be cautious with whom we share our hopes, dreams, and fears. As women, we "naturally" tend to connect with men, and so we must be on guard about our interactions. For you it may be a casual relationship with a counselor, friend, co-worker, or even a minister. Even if you feel the relationship is strictly platonic or professional, one moment of vulnerability (for either of you) is all it takes. We know that the Bible cautions us about who we are connected to or yoked with, and it's for good reason. When you least expect it (and with *whom* you least expect it), those casual interactions can *lead* to emotional, physical, and spiritual bonds that are meant to be shared only with your husband—or in an intentional courtship heading toward marriage. I'm sure that many of you, like me, can attest to pain from past relationships where emotional bonds were formed either too soon or went too deep (or both). Those experiences often left us drained, emotionally wounded, and hinder us from being spiritually and emotionally whole.

2. *A godly woman dresses modestly so that she does not cause men to stumble, and she trains her thought life not to lust after men.* Romans 14:13 underscores this principle: "Therefore we must not pass judgment on one another, but rather determine never

to place an obstacle or a trap before a brother or sister." To put it simply, women must be overly careful about what they wear. The focus of men's interest is physical by nature. They don't need any help from us in conjuring up physical desire. This is definitely an area in which your conviction will evolve and grow as the Holy Spirit speaks to your heart. As you pursue the heart of God, you will find that what may have been acceptable in the past is no longer acceptable to you. Closeness to Christ makes us also question our motives. *Why* do we wear what we wear? What message are we sending? What benefit are we expecting in return? I firmly believe that modesty starts in the heart. If you are genuinely unsure about whether something is modest, ask the advice of women who you know dress appropriately. When in doubt, err on the side of being conservative! Here's a reminder for older ladies (we are all older than somebody!). It is your duty to lovingly, yet boldly, encourage/challenge younger ladies in what they wear—not just talk about them as they walk by. I really wish this happened more often among Christian women today. Every woman that dresses immodestly isn't trying to be sensual, sexual or provocative. Sometimes, she just doesn't know better.

3. *A godly woman guards her heart by not engaging in premature interactions with men without clear direction as to the purpose of the relationship.* "An unmarried woman or a virgin is concerned about the things of the Lord, to be holy both in body and spirit. But a married woman is concerned about the things of the world, how to please her husband" (I Cor. 7:34). As we mentioned earlier in this chapter, women must be extremely careful with the time

they spend with men. That caution doesn't end once you decide to enter a relationship. In fact, we have to be even more cautious when we are dating. Women, we need to be honest with ourselves. There is a reason we are always wondering where a relationship is headed. There is a reason why we often feel frustrated when relationships have no determined path or definition. Don't ignore that desire for direction. We have a natural desire to want to be led. Wait! Did I say we *want* to be led? Yes, I said it. Now, I need you to admit it. We long for a man to set clear, specific direction because it protects our hearts and provides security. It is dangerous to settle for temporary emotional fulfillment when you know that you're in a relationship that is going nowhere. Even if you think you're a tough woman and your life experiences have hardened your emotions, you are still subject to the leading of your heart and can fall prey to its emotional influence. Be bold. Have courage. Get out! If the man you're dating hasn't set any direction for the relationship, it doesn't mean he's bad or evil. But it could be a good indicator that it's time to evaluate the "health" of the relationship. You shouldn't set the direction; that's his job. God values you and you should value yourself. Don't be afraid to hold a man to a standard that doesn't allow for an ambiguous, inconsistent, never-ending relationship. ***CAUTION:*** Be careful of men who over spiriutalize their delay. Sometimes you need to let them "wait on God" by themselves. They can call you when they are ready and hope you are still ready and willing.

4. *A godly woman enters into a relationship with a commitment to sexual purity before marriage.* "Do not be deceived," I Corinthians 15:33 admonishes us, "Bad company corrupts good morals."

How many times have you told yourself that the man you were dating was going to change? Sexual purity is hard enough when both the man and the woman totally embrace God's requirement for it. It's even more difficult when one person in the relationship doesn't fully accept the principle of abstinence. Often, but not always, it is the man who struggles with maintaining purity. You may think that this is a "given" especially when dealing with Christians. Don't be deceived. Many single Christians who love God have yet to surrender this area of their lives to Him. Whatever the case, make sure this is agreed on and understood from the onset of the relationship, and set reasonable boundaries and choose accountability partners that will help you uphold this principle.

5. *A godly woman recognizes that God is at the forefront of her life. Her trust is in God and not in her schemes of how to get a man.* Peter wrote in 1 Peter 3:15a, "But set Christ apart as Lord in your heart". Our minds need to be focused on our one true passion, the Lord and the things that please Him. In order to do this we must be willing to stare loneliness, insecurity, disappointment, and other struggles in the face and declare, "Jesus alone is enough!" Does this sound too spiritual? Well, it's true! How many women have you heard say that they weren't even looking to marry when God gave them a husband? A husband is just one thing God can bless a woman with. There are so many other blessings that are realized when we sincerely become consumed with Christ.

6. *A godly woman trains herself to have a submissive and servant attitude in all her relationships.* Ladies, I can't express how important this

is. I Peter 2:18-21 says that your character of service is tested when you're treated unfairly. This is definitely true in marriage.

One of the reasons it is so difficult for many women to practice submissiveness in marriage is that they have not taken time to practice it anywhere else. Think of how many times our selfish, self-centered thinking gets us in trouble and damages relationships.

> *Is his initiation a move of the flesh or the result of a plan laced in prayer?*

You can practice serving and submitting with girlfriends or family. It may be something as minor as being agreeable when a group is deciding where to eat. It may be something simple like coming to a friend's aid when it will truly inconvenience you. This attitude is something we should embrace <u>before</u> marriage. What you practice as a single woman will be what you take into marriage.

7. *A godly woman recognizes that all men are created in the image of God and therefore should be respected. She rejects disrespecting and complaining about men.* Ephesians 5:33 commands wives to respect their husbands. Here again, what you practice as a single woman will be what you take into marriage. How do you treat the men you interact with at work, church, or among friends? How are the men in your family treated? Seeing men through God's eyes is a refreshing perspective that will affect how you relate to them. We need to embrace the reality that they all need our support, encouragement, and respect. It is what God requires

of us. And regarding relationships and marriage, practice makes perfect!

8. *A godly woman understands that the man is the initiator of relationships and she is the responder.* The examples set forth in the lives of Isaac and Rebekah and in the lives of Hosea and Gomer clearly show that men are required by God to initiate the relationship and women are expected to be the responders. However, when the man does initiate, a woman should clearly understand the precise nature of the relationship he is initiating. Why did he approach you? What is his intention for the relationship? What is his philosophy on relationships? Does he have a vision for himself? Is he interested in protecting your heart? Is his initiation a move of the flesh or the result of a plan laced in prayer? Don't get me wrong. **These aren't the questions you should be asking overtly; however, these are questions that you should keep in your mind to see how he responds in the early stages of your interactions with him.** If these questions remain unanswered for too long, you may be heading into one of those ambiguous relationships we talked about earlier, and the effects of that could be devastating.

Now what's a woman to think? You've got a lot of information to process. Most of it may already be familiar to you but now you need to decide what practical changes you may need to make in your behavior and/or your thinking. I know your heart has certain longings for companionship, commitment, and family because God made us that way. But I also know that you have a desire to honor Him with a heart set on righteousness and a lifestyle to match. Following, is one woman's story of how God shed light on her unhealthy relationship.

one woman's experience
"I Learned the Hard Way"

W hen I was in the 6th grade, our school planned a trip to D. C. I went to a private school where most of the children were affluent and paid for their trip well in advance. That, however, was not my story. Although I had my heart set on this trip, my parents could not afford to pay for it before the final due date. On the final payment date, there was a meeting during lunch where the teacher explained what would happen on the trip and the things that we needed to bring. I was so excited to be in that meeting I could hardly contain it. Even though my parents hadn't been able to pay for the trip, my dad promised me that he would stop by school and bring in the full payment for the trip. So as I sat in the meeting at lunch, I was excited and waiting for my dad to show up. During 5th period, I was still excited and waited for my dad to come. By the end of 7th period, I was worried but knew in my heart that my dad would pick me up from school and pay the money. At 4:00 p.m. my mom picked me up from school and took me home.

I'm over 30 years old now, and I still wonder why my dad never showed up that day. Since that day, I've been *subconsciously waiting for someone to "show up", change my circumstances, and take all the anxiety away.*

We all know that waiting is a lonely activity. To deal with the loneliness, I found quick "fixes" in my male friendships. From the beginning these friendships were "unhealthy" but until a year ago, I didn't realize that I struggled with having close male friends. I just thought I was the girl that had a lot of friends that were guys. These guys were there to hangout, do the manly household tasks, help with my career, listen to my woes, provide a "man's perspective", and serve as dates when needed (you know you can't go to dinner, movies, or concerts alone). Most of all they provided a comfort level that made me feel safe when I was with them. They didn't seem to cause any harm at the time. We never crossed any sexual lines, and we always had an understanding that we were "just friends".

That arrangement worked for me, and my guy friends until one guy, Mark, captured my heart. Initially, I wasn't drawn to him. He was just this guy I met who was headed to join the ranks in the "friend zone". He wasn't overly attractive but he was smart, confident, well groomed, charismatic, and good natured. Somehow, Mark never made it to the "friend zone" and I ended up dating him for three years. I was convinced he was the person I had been waiting on to "show up and take my anxiety away". And he did that—for a while. I was so captivated by Mark that I quit my job, left my family, and moved in with him. Never in a million years did I think I would live with a man that was not my husband. I knew I was settling, but I couldn't say no. We had a great relationship. The only problem was that he had a great relationship with someone else as well. He had met another woman who started out as just a "friend". Mark was everything I wanted and more but when I found out about his other "friend", whom he had been dating since his divorce two years before he met me, I decided it was time to move on.

That relationship only damaged me further. It added to the pain that had been festering since the 6th grade. It took me at least three years to get over it. Then, I met Jason. He was the epitome of tall, dark, and handsome. Jason was someone I could laugh and talk with. He was a statesman, great cook, and all around good guy. He allowed me to drop the burden of being all things to all people and allowed me to lean on him for a little while. He became my therapy and I believed he was making it "all better". In my mind, Jason was perfect except for two things: 1) he wasn't ready for a relationship and 2) he had two other female "friends". I was still a little traumatized from my first mistake with Mark and I couldn't imagine dealing with Jason and his other female friends. Jason and I decided not to date. In my heart, I hoped he would get it together, drop the female friends, and choose only me. It didn't matter that Jason said that he only saw me as a friend or that the intimate part of our relationship was over. It only mattered that he was there whenever I needed him, and that I knew things about him that no one else knew. I felt we had a special friendship, and I didn't want to lose access to him. I decided it was better to be Jason's friend on his terms than to have no contact with him at all. For a second time, I chose to settle for less than what I knew God wanted for me.

What does all this have to do with being a godly woman? It is the highlights of two relationships that taught me a valuable lesson about male/female friendships. Let me be clear. I think that men and women can be friends, but I think it requires a lot of honesty and healthy boundaries. I think it's really hard to be friends when two people are attracted to one another and one of them is lying and saying that the other is just their "friend" in hopes that someday the other person will get a clue. I think many people who call themselves "friends" aren't honest with their true desires and that's why this book is so important.

As singles, we need to be honest with who we are, what we desire, and how our past influences our decisions. We must not allow our desires to make us rush into the dating process too quickly. We need to first make sure we are on the path to becoming healthy individuals or we'll end up hurting ourselves even more (not to mention those with whom we are in a relationship.) Choosing your life companion is serious and you should not let the "friendship game" or past hurts get in the way of establishing healthy relationships.

I've looked for my rescuer in my male friends and in my work. In the midst of it all I learned that my "Rescuer" had been there all the time. Now, my desire is no longer that another "Mark" or "Jason" would rescue me, but that a man of God approaches me, in God's timing. My prayer is that he would do so with a heart humbled by Christ and an inner strength that's rooted in his confidence in God's calling on his life.

I was not the only kid who missed out on that 6th grade field trip. Several other kids did not get to go on the trip. We stayed behind and did mundane work while everyone else went away to have fun. Sometimes being single is a lot like that. You watch your friends "go away" to be married while you remain behind.

As disappointing as that may be at times, I'm still trusting God to send His choice for me. In the meantime, I focus on fostering healthy relationships with females and allowing God to heal me from past hurts so that I become a restored, emotionally whole vessel that He can use for His work.

who's your comforter?

4

opeye had his spinach, George Burns had his cigars, and Linus had his blanket. What or who do you use to feel secure or comforted? What do you do when you are lonely, frustrated, confused, angry, stressed, bored, or when you simply want to be loved? Conway loves to play soccer or go for a jog when he needs to relieve a little stress. I (Jada) often use a good jog to clear my mind as well. Sometimes insecurity leads me to the mall to "treat myself". It makes me feel a *little* better for a *little* while. Who or what is your substitute for God during these bad days? What do you do to quench your thirst when life leaves you feeling a little parched? Is God really enough for you? I want to encourage you to let Him bring you full satisfaction in every situation.

"On the last day of the feast, the greatest day, Jesus stood up and shouted out, 'If anyone is thirsty, let him come to me'" (John 7:37). Jesus was talking to a group of people who, by no means, should have been thirsty. The context was the *last* day of a *great feast*. These people had been eating and drinking for days. The last day of this feast was also traditionally the day of reflection. Jesus wanted to share parting words that they would carry home. He decided to stand on *an elevation* and He decided to shout *a proclamation*. He wanted their attention.

His declaration has three key words. The first key word is "if," which presents a condition. Jesus knew that some of the people listening to Him were not going to believe or realize that they were in fact thirsty. The second key word in Christ's statement is "come." This is an action word that indicates initiative. It's critical to consider this because the initiative falls on the pronoun "him" which represents the thirsty person. The third key word is "Me," which represents where the thirsty person is to go. So in verse 37, we see Jesus giving the people an opportunity to (1) consider their condition and determine if they are thirsty, (2) take action once that thirst is realized, and (3) understand that the solution is in Christ.

What are they thirsty for? That's what I asked when I first read this passage. Based on Jesus' response in verse 38, they are thirsty for something that never runs out. These people didn't just need the drink He offered in verse 37; they needed the renewable resources He offered in verse 38. Do you know that because we are all created in God's image, we all have a thirst for something that never runs out? That something, that some*One*, is God. If you have accepted Christ as your Savior by grace alone, through faith alone, you already have the "flow" that Jesus refers to in verse 38. However, on a regular day-to-day basis, are you tapping into it or are you using substitutes? Serious problems arise when we try to quench this thirst for something deep, meaningful, and eternal with something shallow, meaningless, and temporary, hoping that the cumulative effect will be something great.

Is Christ alone enough for you? Is His love and affection for you enough to quench your thirst? If your life is characterized by contentment, the answer to this question is yes. If you struggle with choosing joy, even during hard times (James 1:2), or if God is not the first person you run to when you need comfort, the answer for you is probably no. Most of us find ourselves in the "no" category. When we use our own devices to soothe our hurt, it breaks God's heart. God lamented when the Israelites resorted to other means of contentment when He said, "...my people have committed a

> **When we use our own devices to soothe our hurt, it breaks God's heart.**

double wrong: they have left me, the fountain of life-giving water, and they have dug cisterns for themselves, cracked cisterns which cannot even hold water" (Jer. 2:13). They had again chosen to build idols to worship in place of God. God equated those idols to "broken cisterns." Cisterns were made for carrying water from a well to a certain destination, but if a cistern was broken or cracked in any way, there would be little to no water by the time the carrier reached his destination. The carrier of a broken cistern would be in the same condition (no water) he was in *before* his trip to the well—actually a worse condition because of the time and energy expended only to return empty.

Our list of comforts—shopping, dates, <u>relationships</u>, workouts, friends, vacations, parties, movies, food, sleep, "vegging out," alcohol, drugs, music, and the all-powerful "idiot box" (television)—can become our broken cisterns when we try to use them to hold water that will quench our thirst. Haven't you noticed that after you've done whatever you do to "take your mind off things" that you're still left with these unresolved issues? What broken cisterns are you spending energy carrying that aren't providing you with any benefit? Only when we embrace the sovereignty of God, and believe what He says about His love for us and His plan for our lives, can we join the apostle Paul in saying, "I am not saying this because I am in need, for I have learned to be content in any circumstance. I have experienced times of need and times of abundance. In any and every circumstance I have learned the secret of contentment, whether I go satisfied or hungry, have plenty or nothing" (Phil. 4:11-12).

You may be asking, "Why should I face my comforts? Who cares? What does this have to do with dating or relationships?" To answer these questions, let's first begin with the point that God hates it. In other words, He dislikes anything that is used as a substitute for Him. He calls it evil, which means it's a sin. Second, it hinders intimacy with God. In Jeremiah 2, God is angry because His people have built idols to worship in place of Him. Worship is the expression of our intimacy with God and that intimacy is hampered when we use meaningless replacements for God. Third, it will never completely satisfy us. John 7 shows Jesus still addressing the same issue which God had to chastise His people about thousands of years earlier. If these substitutes or comforters really worked, we would not still be thirsty after we used them. Have you noticed that the "comforters" we use have serious, diminishing returns? The more often we use them, the more we need.

Fourth, we need to face the comforters in our lives because if we don't, it may lead to unhealthy addictions. One drink doesn't make an alcoholic. One bet doesn't make a compulsive gambler. One desperate phone call to a friend doesn't make a person codependent. We reach the intensity and frequency that define addiction one small step at a time, so we must constantly check our motives for why we do what we do. We must continuously ask ourselves if we're forming unhealthy habits which lead to life-controlling addictions, even if no one else can see them.

The reality is it's the only way we can passionately pursue God for *who* He is and not *what* He can give us. For many singles, marriage is simply another potential "comforter" that they believe will magically bring them the contentment they should be finding in God. Do you fit into this category? Why would God bless you with one of His sons or daughters as a mate, when He knows that you would use that person as a substitute thirst-quencher? We set ourselves and potential mates up for failure when our lack of contentment forces them to meet needs they are incapable of meeting. The antidote to pursuing comforters and substitutes is contentment. Most of us live in one of two "tents" – contentment or discontentment. The question is in which tent do you live? One of the primary reasons marriages fail is the inability of spouses to be content in the situations that God allows in their lives.

Not sure which tent you live in? Ask yourself *why* you want to be married. If you desire marriage (or a dating relationship) as a cure for something (loneliness, love, friendship/companionship), you might have an unhealthy viewpoint. Think about how you would respond if you were somehow to find out that you will never be married. What if you were going to be married for less than five years before your spouse became terminally ill or died. If these thoughts make you cringe, you may be using the idea of marriage as a broken cistern.

We all know people who are never satisfied. The first sin committed by mankind was rooted in discontentment. Adam and Eve weren't satisfied with God's provision in the Garden of Eden. They had everything they could possibly need but they wanted the one thing they couldn't have. It became their focus and ultimately their downfall. Their lack of contentment forced them to miss out on the ultimate intimate relationship and communion with God. The devil uses the same strategy against singles today that he used against Adam and Eve in the beginning. He simply distracts them and gets them to focus on the thing they do not have (a mate) and plants seeds of discontentment that in the end will cause them to miss out on the many things they do have. Things like flexibility, freedom, unrestricted resources, and availability for ministry are just a few of the things God specifically gives singles.

What can you do to avoid falling into the traps of your own flesh, the devil, and the world? You should make it your goal to cultivate the contentment and joy that Paul encourages the Philippians to have.

What can we learn from God's Word on how to cultivate contentment?

1. <u>Believe that God knows you best (Ps. 139:1-13).</u> One of the most comforting thoughts is knowing that God is intimately acquainted with all of our ways. To know that God knows our thoughts and our every move provides an overwhelming sense of security. No one else can know us and accept us the way God does.

2. <u>Trust that God has a plan for your life and it is in your BEST interest (Jer. 29:11).</u> Every time we doubt our life circumstances we ultimately doubt God. Notice the word "circumstances" is quite different from the word "consequences." Consequences are the results of our own sinful actions and poor decisions. Although God can use our consequences also, our *circumstances* are the things we usually don't have control over. We need to trust God after broken relationships, lay-offs, and loss of loved ones. When no one seems to be interested in our lives, when we don't feel attractive, when we aren't as successful as we want to be, and when the dream of fulfillment we seek seems to keep getting delayed, we must believe what God says in Jeremiah 29:11, and trust that He has a plan for our success and not our failure.

3. <u>Praise God for who He is and who He made you to be (Ps. 139:14-17).</u> In Psalm 139 David is thankful because God has made him fearfully and wonderfully. It brought David joy and gratefulness simply to reflect that God had uniquely crafted him. If you genuinely believe that your Creator took great care in "forming"

you, then you have just accepted the ultimate compliment and the greatest affirmation. The diluted affirmations that the world, the enemy, and your flesh offer will dwarf in significance.

4. <u>**Know that you are growing and making progress (Phil. 1:6; 2:13).**</u> So often we look at our lives and beg God for a little bit of progress or some sign of growth. One of the most frustrating things is feeling like you're expending energy without results. But Philippians 1:6 assures us that God is still working on us from *within* so we don't have to chase after the world's icons of success. Without the latest car, newest home, or trendiest wardrobe God is still doing a "good work" in us.

5. <u>**Ask (*and allow*) God to remove the wrong motives for substitutes from your heart (Ps. 139:23 -34).**</u> After David spent time reflecting on the amazing intimacy he had with God and how well God knew him, he then asked God to search his heart. David wanted to be sure that any wrong thoughts were removed so he could fully embrace righteousness. We have to surrender our hearts to God and ask Him to search us. Anxious thoughts, as the psalmist calls them, become fertile ground for discontentment and are often at the root of the deceptions that lead us to seek out substitutes for God.

6. <u>**Think on things that are right (Phil. 4:8; Rom. 8:6-7).**</u> The apostle Paul says a mind set on things of the flesh is death but a mind set on the Spirit is life and peace. We all know that our minds must be subject to the things of Christ. We must meditate on things that are true, pure, lovely, excellent, honorable, right, of

good repute, and praiseworthy. Whew! That doesn't leave room for much else – and that, my friend, is the point.

7. **<u>Hang around contented people who can encourage you (Job 6:14; Prov. 17:17).</u>** Biblical wisdom contends that a man's friends should bring kindness when he in is despair and that friends should love at all times. Friends who love at all times will provide godly support and encouragement when we face moments of weakness. We need people, with whom we have authentic relationships, to help us when we are too vulnerable to help ourselves. If you want to move from discontentment to contentment, you've got to have friends who can help you make the journey.

When we begin to choose joy and contentment instead of allowing our feelings and circumstances to dictate our behavior, we start to see God in a brand new way. This new perspective not only draws us closer to Him, it also helps us to have realistic expectations for everything else in our lives including our dating relationships and ultimately our marriage.

experiencing healthy relationships 5

We live in a world where physical and emotional promiscuity is very prevalent. Guys engage in unhealthy, codependent relationships with women. Women hold on to men who do not desire a commitment. We now have a culture where individuals simply date to marry rather than marry to date. We want the benefits of marriage without the responsibility and the commitment of marriage. That's why many people get so emotionally connected during the dating process and that's why they are so devastated when the relationship ends. This type of connectivity was designed for marriage, not for a casual dating relationship. But how do we solve this problem?

The disintegration of the institution of marriage has led to our culture losing one of its most powerful images—relationships thriving in a healthy environment. The result instead is that we have models of unhealthy, codependent, sometimes abusive, and self-centered relationships. With poor family models, our culture then decides what is right and what is wrong not based on God's Word but on what feels good and what satisfies oneself. What impact does this have on today's singles?

It definitely impacted the relationship I (Conway) described in chapter one. I prioritized my feelings and my needs over hers. In the final phase of this journey I was on, I identified seven biblical truths that brought me closer to seeing relationships and marriage the way God designed them.

First, Genesis 2:15-18 indicates that men are to be initiators and women are the responders. It's important that men understand their God-given role as initiators. The truth is, the choice Adam made to follow Eve's initiation and eat the forbidden fruit put them and us under a curse. It reversed the roles of a man and a woman and we are suffering from the effects of it to this day. Many women try to carry the burden of leadership and men willingly take on a passive role. Even the way families are personified on television and in movies reinforce this role reversal. We do not often see a family in which the husband is clearly the leader and the wife respects him as such. If we are to turn the tide on unhealthy relationships, we must first reverse this. Men must embrace their God-given role to initiate, direct, and lead, and women must accept their God-given role to support, enhance, and connect as God leads.

I also realized that I needed to focus intentionally on developing healthy male friendships. Daniel demonstrates this principle when he developed these relationships with Hananiah, Mishael, Azariah (Daniel 1). We naturally form bonds with the opposite sex and those "friendships" seem so easy to maintain. Learning to have meaningful, long-term friendships with people of your same sex forces you to deal with a lot of issues that you can avoid in friendships with the opposite sex. There's no chemistry and no mystery. In order for same-sex friendships to last, it takes old-fashioned hard work, and consistency.

Why? Because men are not impressed with how another man looks. They relate to each other based on character and not on emotions or external qualities. Some women have difficulty relating with other women because they are judged based on their character and selflessness and not on beauty or talents. When men have brothers who are their best friends and accountability partners, it forces them to be men of integrity and exhibit the fruit of the Spirit in their relationships. Similarly, when women have close girlfriends with whom they confide, they are forced to be more aware of whom they are and of the internal issues they need to work on and develop.

It takes far more "spiritual" work to develop healthy relationships with the same sex than it does with the opposite sex, but it is an incredible developmental tool for growing in the areas of flexibility, awareness, teachability, and faithfulness. Many men only have female friends and many women only have male friends. It is often said that men can't trust other men because of their pride, and women can't trust other women because they love to be 'catty' or petty and emotional. The reality is that it is simply easier to have opposite-sex 'best friends' because there is always a mystery and chemistry that surrounds such a relationship, but having authentic friendships within the same sex is more difficult and rare.

During this process I was reminded of the principle of selflessness. It is a crucial factor to the success of a healthy relationship (Philippians 2:1-5). People are driven by many forces today. Some people are driven by fear and some by pride. Still others are driven by success. But seldom is the motivation to exalt or lift up the other person. People are more concerned with making themselves better than with making someone else better. As Christians in relationships, we should consistently consider others above ourselves. In James 4:1, we learn that the reason for poor relationships and conflicts is our flawed motives and self-centeredness. Therefore, in order to lead the turnaround from unhealthy to healthy relationships, we must cultivate the habit of selflessness and genuinely prioritize others above ourselves.

Living by faith was another principle God reinforced in me (Hebrews 11:6). We all have a consistent tendency to live by sight and not by faith when selecting a mate or pursuing a relationship. We crave instant gratification and that requires that we primarily trust what we can see and touch. For this reason, many men argue that they have to "test" a woman for a couple years before they can commit or many women argue that they have to see the man in all the seasons before they can make any kind of commitment. The problem with this type of thinking is that it's all about sight, not about faith. The Bible says without faith it is impossible to please God.

When it's time to select a mate most of you probably have a "list". That list is supposed to capture all of the "must haves" regarding the characteristics of a potential spouse. Anytime you meet someone that has qualities from your list, you probably begin to wonder if they might be "the one". That type of thinking seems to leave God out of the equation. Anything can happen at anytime to change the ideal scenario. That is why we don't have to date for a year or two to see how the relationship is going to work, nor do we have to know everything about someone to make up our minds. A part of the decision is the faith factor. We must do all the observation and evaluation without getting the emotions involved or engaging the heart, and then we must trust God to move us forward by faith and with wisdom.

Proverbs 27:6 tells us, "Faithful are the wounds of a friend, but the kisses of an enemy are excessive." This simply means that a real friend will tell you what you need to hear – not just what you want to hear. This is accountability at its best and I learned first hand how important it is. If I had allowed more people to hold me accountable, they would have questioned the intent and direction of my relationship (chapter 1) from the beginning. A strong support/ accountability system is paramount to healthy relationships. True accountability is rare in our culture because we always want to be the master of our destiny and we often lack the courage to speak truth into one another's life. But true life change really happens best when we have a small group of friends, that love God and share our values for righteousness, and who will challenge and encourage us when life happens. To truly enjoy the benefits of accountability relationships, we must be willing to be vulnerable and open. If we are going to change the trend of poor relationships, we must connect with a group of like-minded individuals that will hold us accountable to our new value system and to living differently in a warped culture.

Contentment (as we mentioned earlier) is another foundational element of having a balanced relationship that pleases God. In a world that is suffering from chronic discontentment, healthy relationships are cultivated in the soil of contentment. If you are single and unsatisfied, chances are you will be married and unsatisfied. Satisfaction comes from our relationship with God not from our marital status – or any other life circumstance. The apostle Paul in Philippians 4:11, argues,

"… for I have learned to be content in any circumstance." This means that God was enough for Paul. Not God plus something. God alone was enough for Paul. If you begin to embrace Paul's thinking, you will begin to see your relationship or future relationship in a much more balanced light with more realistic expectations.

Finally, our love for God must be preeminent over all. Our love for God should be a supreme love (Matt. 10:37). If we just exist, we will be caught up in loving the world, and all of its messages, more than we love God. The world around us is rapidly going downstream and God has called us to go against the grain and swim upstream. The world's lure is so appealing that most of us are simply following its direction without even knowing it. Choosing to love God more than the world is all about consumption. What are you consumed with? Work? Friends? Status? Appearance? If you're not sure, take a look at your bank statement. Where do you spend your money? Take a look at your planner. Where do you spend your time? When God is our first love, He has first dibs on our resources, time, body and mind.

If you begin to look for ways to apply these truths to your life, you can ignite a revolution of developing strong, loving, and healthy

relationships with an approach based on biblical values.

But what about the subtle issues that threaten to disrupt the cultivation of healthy relationships? How do men and women relate to each other in a God-honoring way? How does a man treat a woman like a sister with all purity? How can men and women guard their hearts? How can singles avoid the hurt and the pain that so often plague Christians in relationships?

The Bible often uses relationships among family members to describe how the body of Christ ought to relate to one another. One scripture reference for this principle can be found in I Timothy 5:1-2, where the apostle Paul writes, "Do not address an older man harshly but appeal to him as a father. Speak to younger men as brothers, older women as mothers, and younger women as sisters—with complete purity." Brothers, from a relational standpoint, we are to treat women we come in contact with as we would our own sister. Would you romance your sister? Would you give her gifts that entice her to invest her emotions in you without commitment? Would you caress and kiss your sister? Would you have sexual relations with her? To do so would go against God's Word in Leviticus 18:6-9, "'No man is to approach any close relative to have sexual relations with her..." The King James Version reads, "The nakedness of thy sister...thou shall not uncover."

Although I did not have sexual relations with the young woman from the first chapter, I did not treat her with the purity I would treat my own sister. Ultimately, I did not grasp the power of protecting her heart. Now that's a powerful principle. How does a man protect a woman's heart and not hurt her in the dating process?

Psalm 141:3 says, "O Lord, place a guard on my mouth! Protect the opening of my lips." Even though it is helpful to think of each other as siblings, that doesn't mean we share everything we would share with a brother or sister. Does that make sense? Some dating couples talk so freely about marriage, children and a house that they begin to assume commitment when there is none. Once this line has been crossed and the relationship ends, the woman often feels cheated, as she looks back, and the man usually feels misunderstood. Brothers, as the initiators, you have a responsibility to guard a woman's heart at all times during your interactions with her. Sisters, you have a responsibility to "Guard your heart with all vigilance, for from it are the sources of life." (Prov. 4:23).

The task of guarding your heart means to keep from turning your emotions over to someone who might be found untrustworthy. Whether the commitment is in the context of the accountability groups mentioned earlier, or for marriage, your heart should only be available to people who genuinely care about you and seek your best interest. Another term for guarding the heart is emotional abstinence. Martha Ruppert suggests in her book <u>The Dating Trap</u>,

> *"Emotional abstinence means we do not allow our emotions to be manipulated, nor do we use our emotions to manipulate others. It means we do not give our hearts away to any number of people as we await a wedding day. Christians aren't supposed to rely on emotions as a compass to guide our lives. Yet we have the misconception*

that if we are guarded about our emotions, then we are not loving, and the chance at love may pass us by. Of course romance and love are not wrong. But neither are they supposed to be recreational activities. Being emotionally vulnerable is not something we practice so we will be ready for marriage. Vulnerability is something we protect so we will be prepared to give freely in marriage."

In order to practice emotional abstinence you can use some of these practical precautions:

1. **Be selective about what areas of your life you expose others to (family, church, special occasions, etc.).** Some areas of our lives should require a level of commitment before we grant access to others. Sharing very personal experiences too early with others can create a false sense of maturity and intimacy in a relationship. As soon as you feel betrayed, these experiences will be the first things you'll regret.

2. **Be discerning about sharing intimate emotions.** Your deepest fears, intimate prayer requests, dreams, and insecurities are treasures to be given cautiously to people who are choosing to journey with you over the long haul.

3. **When relating to men, take what they say at face value.** Men generally <u>mean what they say.</u> Ladies, if you are dating a man and he says, "I'm not ready for commitment" that means he's not ready for commitment. If you choose to proceed with

the relationship hoping to change his mind, you will be sorely disappointed when it's all said and done. There's nothing you can do to change his mind but there is a lot you can do to control yours. Use wisdom and wise counsel to help manage the tendency to take things further in your mind than they may be in reality. (*i.e. don't visualize the wedding on the first date!*)

4. **When relating to women, read between the lines**. That doesn't mean that you should make up things that don't exist. It just means that if a woman says something, her behavior should be consistent with what she says. If it's not, you may need to challenge her on what she expressed verbally. Women will say things that they think a man wants to hear – and in reality it may be a misrepresentation of how they really feel. (*i.e. if she says she only likes you as a friend but questions where you go and who you spend your time with – you need to read between the lines!*)

Joshua Harris, the author of the books *I Kissed Dating Goodbye, Boy Meets Girl,* and *Sex Is Not the Problem (Lust Is)*, wrote, "The job of guarding our hearts is a big responsibility. It takes place in the secret places of devotion. In honest prayer and meditation on God's Word, we scrape the film of infatuation, lust and self-pity from our hearts…The work is never done. We must police our hearts with faithful, silent regularity."

Remember, we help guard the hearts of others by not luring them into trusting us with their minds, wills, and emotions before we are committed to their welfare.

an illustration:
engaging the heart
One Couple's Experience

I n February 2005 I was a content single female who was truly enjoying what God was doing in my life. I was traveling the country as a consultant and was loving all the freedom and independence that I had. My singleness was a gift and I was thoroughly enjoying it – I wasn't looking for a boyfriend. I believed that God would one day bless me with a mate (my plan was for that to happen in at least four years) but I made a decision to trust and obey the Lord even if He never gave me a husband. It was during this month that I sat down and talked with Conway for the first time. I shared my testimony, discussed ways I could serve in the Singles Ministry, and then somehow started talking about relationships. He asked me about my "Dating Requirements List" and challenged me to revise it. You know the list, the one that almost every girl has that describes, in detail, all the characteristics a man must have in order to even have a chance in dating her. I, of course, had "being a Christian" as the number one requirement and then other stipulations regarding annual salary, level of education, height, and ability to speak proper English. Conway's challenge to me was to make all the "requirements" biblical and to *make sure that they would lead to a successful marriage.*

He even challenged me to narrow my list (which was well over 10 requirements) down to 3! I told him that would be impossible, but after a lot of complaining, I revised my list. I eventually got the list down to fulfilling the Great Commandment and the Great Commission: "Jesus said to him, **"'Love the Lord your God with all your heart, with all your soul, and with all your mind**. This is the first and greatest commandment. The second is like it: '**Love your neighbor as yourself**" *(Matthew 22:37, 39) and "Therefore go and make disciples of all nations" (Matthew 28:19). I then waited patiently to see what the Lord would do.*

In the summer of 2004, I was introduced to Mr. T. through mutual friends. I learned about his involvement in the Plumbline ministry at UNT and became a big fan of his music. I was truly impressed with his heart of service and thought that he was an awesome man of God, concluding that he'd make someone a good husband one day. After really only having known Mr. T. as a friend of a friend, a more relevant friendship emerged between us in July 2005. I was in Golden, Missouri serving as a volunteer counselor at Kids Across America, and he was there as well for a Fourth of July concert. I found out later that he noticed my service and saw certain qualities in me that sparked his interest. Before approaching me, he asked people at camp that knew me well – our mutual friends, other counselors, and even the camp director – about my character and what kind of person I was.

After getting back a "positive report" he began his pursuit. He called me at the end of July with the hopes of getting to know me better. I was excited that this guy was calling me, but wouldn't let myself draw conclusions that weren't based on reality. I decided to think on those things that were true, noble and trustworthy (Phil 4:8), and what was true for me was that we were nothing more than friends. We got to know one another better through talking on the phone and hanging out together at the mall once. I told my girlfriends and accountability partners about my new friend and they encouraged me to make sure my motivations for allowing him to engage me in conversation were pure and that we were being wise with the amount of time we talked on the phone. I listened. Having made mistakes in the past of pursuing a man, I was careful to not pursue him. I chose to guard my heart by allowing him to initiate conversations and times to hang out. He was going to have to pursue me.

After a few weeks of being friends, he made his intentions clear – he shared that he was interested in pursuing a relationship with me, a relationship that would hopefully lead to a courtship and end in marriage. He shared his feelings for me and told me about the qualities he had observed in me over time. It was then my turn to observe Mr. T. more so that I could make the decision of whether or not I truly wanted to engage in a courtship with him.

Having already observed all the qualities on my revised "Dating Requirements List," I asked people in his life about his character and had asked him to meet with Conway, my spiritual covering, so that Conway could check him out for me and validate his character. For a month I watched him in service and observed the "5 timeless traits" (Faithfulness, Awareness, Initiative, Teachable and Humility before God) in Mr. T. and in September 2005 we decided to enter into a courtship, praying that it would end in marriage.

During our courtship we each individually met with Conway, his pastor and other married couples in our lives that served as mentor couples. We read a book together called "Define the Relationship" that offers advice to guide couples through dating. With biblical teaching it helps couples end their dating relationships – either with breaking up or with engagement – successfully. This book guided us through developing physical and emotional boundaries, resolving conflict, discussing past sins, and periodically evaluating our relationship to ensure that we both were still on the same track to marriage. As we continued to grow as a couple we faced many struggles – including finances, jobs, the desire for children, and familial conflict. Having lived as "Miss Independent" for so long I struggled with the idea of submission, and the roles that the Lord has given men and women in marriage. The root issues of many of our arguments were selfishness, impatience, lack of confidence in the Lord's sovereignty, pride, and the lack of willingness to deny self.

During our relationship we were diligent in prayer, Bible study, and we sought godly counsel from those around us so that we would be able to discern God's pleasing and perfect will for our lives (Romans 12:2). **Many times we wanted to give up; I know I wanted to walk away on many different occasions because things weren't going as I expected. Mr. T. and I didn't seem to be compatible and I was miserable.** *Initially, I resented Conway for asking me to change my "Dating Requirements List." I later learned that we couldn't cling to compatibility – we had to cling to Christ. In March 2006, after lots of joy, fun, trials, tests, fasting and praying, we made the decision to join together in marriage – convinced that we could together, as one, glorify the Lord and do more for His kingdom than we could do separately as singles. We weren't officially engaged until May 2006, but we committed ourselves in March to prepare for a wedding, and more importantly – a marriage.*

got f.a.i.t.h.?6

What's next? This might be what you're asking as you progress on the journey of becoming who God has called you to be, grasping the principles in understanding what it means to be a godly man or woman, and recognizing the importance of guarding your heart. More specifically, men may be asking, "How do I find the woman God has called to be my helpmate?" Ladies, you may be asking, "How do I recognize the man God has called to be my husband?" Before we answer those questions let's first look at the problems with our current approaches to dating.

The problem with dating strategies is that they often don't provide any objective guidelines for couples to adhere to. Compatibility is only a part of the equation, and according to God it isn't the most significant part. There are many questions facing singles who are in the dating process today. Here are a few:

- How and where will I find my potential mate?

- How many of my preferences should I "hold out" for?

- Is the person I am dating a phony or the real deal?

- Is the person just performing? Will everything change after the wedding?

- If he or she is having sex with me now and violating God's guidelines, what proof do I have that he or she will be faithful after we get married?

- Why does it seem as if everyone I date is flaky (noncommittal) and does not share the same values I do?

- How long should a dating relationship last before you make a decision for marriage?

- How can I look at a person's current life and determine if he or she will make a good mate?

- What do I do if I don't have Christian parents or a Christian model to follow?

Our culture tells us to do what feels right, judge the book by its cover, test the merchandise before we buy, and spend more time on the wedding than the marriage. If none of that works then you can justify divorce with "irreconcilable differences." What is clear in our culture is that the current dating approaches are leading to a divorce rate of over 50 percent. In order to change these devastating results, we must examine what happens before we enter marriage, not simply why we stop liking each other after marriage.

The following processes (one for men and one for women)

are designed to help singles customize an approach that will assist them in avoiding the games people play in dating and allow them to embrace a general plan to help them think through the dating/ courting process from a divine perspective.

WHO is this for? Men

WHAT is their role? Pursuers (*Men are to initiate the relationship*)

WHAT should they do?

1. *Be Under a "Covering"* (have a mentor/spiritual father). In the ideal situation singles should have parents who provide wisdom and direction. If this is not the case, then you should seek wisdom and direction from a mentor and a spiritual father.

2. *Identify Timeless Traits.* This is the "list." What are you looking for in a mate? Before you meet someone, you should identify not just *preferences* but *principles* the Bible supports. (We will address this in the second half of this chapter.)

> *... if the relationship does not lead to marriage, she should be better off for having known you, not regretting the day she met you.*

3. *Observe*. Without her knowing that you are observing her, look to see if she possesses the timeless traits you've identified. Ask her friends, people she doesn't get along with, family, ministry leaders, and associates questions related to her character. If you wait to try and observe these traits after you meet her, then you will have a hard time being objective and you may run the risk of her performing to please you and/or being hurt if you become uninterested.

4. *Make Contact*. Approach the woman you've observed with a plan in mind and recognize that she has not yet had the opportunity to observe you. Don't scare her or stalk her. If she doesn't want to meet with you, move on. You certainly don't want to force a relationship.

5. *"Engage" Her Heart*. The more you interact with and speak to her you must recognize that it is very likely that her heart is being engaged or emotionally invested (even if she doesn't admit it). Even so, the interaction can be done in a considerate and respectful way. As the man, you now have the responsibility to continue to treat her like a sister until she accepts the invitation, which leads to

courtship. Think of it this way—if the relationship does not lead to marriage, she should be better off for having known you, not regretting the day she met you.

6. *Enter a Courtship* (with an agreed—upon, specific timeline). After you've gotten permission from her covering and there is an agreement to continue toward courtship, then, you must set clear direction, so that she never has to guess or wonder about your intentions and or a general timeframe for the relationship. This phase means that both people agree that marriage is the destination. The wedding date can be set because the proposal could happen at any time. Ideally a mentor couple is identified (if this hasn't already happened) to help navigate the way.

7. *Get Engaged.* Obviously, this is when you ask the big question. Guys, when you ask this question you should already be certain of the answer. During this stage you and your fiancée may choose to make more permanent decisions regarding career, finances, family, etc. But continue to be careful. Until you are married, you are still separate in God's eyes. (Seek out premarital counseling)

8. *Get Married.* Now the real work begins!

9. *Continue to Meet with Your Mentor Couple.* Regular meetings should be set up with your mentor couple. If problems arise, either individual should feel free to contact the mentor couple for help.

WHO is this for? Women

WHAT is their role? Responders (*Men initiate the relationship*)

WHAT should they do?

1. *Be Under a "Covering."* This should be a person you respect and admire. An individual whom you trust and whose wisdom is consistent with biblical principles (see chapter 3 for details).

2. *Identify Timeless Traits.* Think through the traits you desire to see in your potential mate. You probably already have a "list," but is it driven by biblical principles that make great marriages or just your preferences?

3. *Introduce Your Covering:* If someone approaches you, <u>and you are interested</u> (don't force interest but also be open to God bringing your mate in an unexpected package) introduce the person to your spiritual father/spiritual parents. Your spiritual father (or the couple) might be aware of things that you are either blind to or have just overlooked.

4. *Observe.* Observe the man for your timeless traits. Measure him against your new and improved list. Ask his friends, people he's not so friendly with, family, ministry leaders, and associates questions related to your traits. This will help you see if his good behavior is authentic or just a show!

5. *Consult Your Covering.* Continuously meet with your spiritual

father/parents to discuss the process, the progress of the relationship, and the emotions involved.

6. *Make a Decision Together.* After discussing the relationship with the man pursuing you, resist the desire to be exclusive too early. Be sure to include your mentor or covering and after much prayer and reflection (you can't have too much of this!), make the decision.

7. *Enter a Courtship.* This is of course initiated by the man. You should receive clear direction from the man, and most importantly, make sure that you enjoy the process! Remember, at this phase, for all intents and purposes, you are engaged. The formal proposal could come at any time.

8. *Marriage.* The real work begins! (Set aside extra time for a devotional quiet time. You're going to need it!)

9. *Continue to Meet with Your Mentor Couple.* Regular meetings should be set up between couples. If problems arise, either you or your spouse should feel free to contact the mentor couple for help.

Identifying Timeless Traits

Aaaaahhh. You were probably wondering when we were going to get to this part. This is where we discuss what goes on that "list" that you should use to measure the man or woman you're interested in.

One of the keys to a successful marriage is not only becoming the right person but also learning to identify the right mate. But what characteristics do you look for? Often singles look for people who compliment them or people who they believe will help them have a better future, but they overlook the timeless traits that make a healthy marriage. They get caught up in things that might change such as physical appearance, financial status, and professional and educational background. Now don't get me wrong, these qualities aren't to be ignored completely, but they are definitely fleeting and won't serve as the bedrock of a lasting, healthy marriage.

The "list" has less to do with your personal preference and more to do with what makes a healthy marriage. Abraham's servant looked for a young lady with a servant's heart (a woman that would offer water to his animals) for his master's son Isaac (Gen. 24). Not once did he ask God for her to be beautiful. Likewise, we should prioritize a person's character over their outward appearance.

All it takes is F.A.I.T.H.

The word "faith" occurs more than 230 times in the New Testament. More than 40 of those occurrences are direct words from Jesus. It's what He is most impressed with, and He often rebuked His disciples for their lack of it. Throughout the Bible, faith is the direct cause of healing, blessing, and salvation, whereas the lack of faith is directly related to doubt, worry, and fear. We use the word "faith" as an acrostic for identifying lasting qualities in potential mates. Remember that everything you look for in someone else must be something you value yourself. So first ask yourself, "Do I have F.A.I.T.H?"

F.A.I.T.H. is **F**aithfulness, **A**wareness, **I**nitiative (for the men), **I**ntentional responsiveness (for the women), **T**eachability, and **H**umility before God. Over the next few pages, we'll discuss each of these in more detail.

Faithfulness *(Matt. 17:20)*

This quality of faithfulness is twofold. First, faithfulness relates to whether the person is a Christian. You cannot begin to assess how a person lives his life if you are not absolutely certain that he or she has trusted Christ as his Savior. It is amazing how often singles try to skip this step and focus on all the "good" qualities a person may exhibit. However, all the goodness in the world is meaningless if a person is not a Christian. Moreover, it is unfair to expect someone who isn't saved to consistently embrace and model the characteristics of believers. The second aspect of faithfulness has to do with a person's trustworthiness and dependability. You need to know if the person you're considering as a mate values commitment and integrity. A person's ability to stick with situations and keep his word, even when it's difficult, is a person who is ready to face some of the many challenges that will arise in marriage. Does the person you're evaluating quit things before he/she finishes them? Does the person follow through on commitments and promises or is the person known for being "flaky"?

Awareness *(Matt. 26:34-35)*

Have you ever been driving down the street and seen a car that had the gas door open or a person who had his seatbelt or her dress dragging underneath the driver's door? Don't you wish you could make them aware of it so they could correct it? Awareness is the quality of understanding self. It means that the individual is clued in to his/her areas of weakness and strength.

Like the drivers with the dangling seatbelts or open gas doors, we all have issues everyone else can see. The question is whether we can see our own issues. You should place priority on understanding who you are and who you are not, what you're great at, and what you struggle with. Expect the same for someone you might enter a relationship with. When a person is not aware and not honest about who he/she is, there is often blame placed on people and circumstances for what happens in his/her life, instead of being personally responsible for actions and decisions. Such a person often misses out on opportunities for personal and spiritual growth. People who lack self-awareness are usually clueless as to how their behavior impacts those around them. In Matthew 26:34-35, Jesus told Peter that he would deny Him as Lord three times before the cock would crow. Peter, lacking self-awareness, adamantly denied this claim. Peter had such an unclear picture of who he was that he actually argued against something that Jesus said was true! When we suffer from a lack of self-understanding, we can convince ourselves that we are better than we actually are and that prevents us from being able to grow in grace.

Initiative *(Matt. 9:2)*

By now you know that we believe that men should never embrace a passive way of living. Life is too short and the call of Christ too great for us not to be initiative takers. To clarify, we need to take the initiative in obedience to God's Word and not in fulfilling the desires of our flesh. That means that women should be looking to see if a man actively pursues Christ and His plan for his life. She should observe whether or not he takes the initiative in living for Christ (evangelism, service, righteousness, etc). Does he graciously yet firmly take on a leadership role, even if that means he's leading through serving? These are the things Christ asked us to do. Most men have no problem doing this in their careers, education, and finances, but what about being first to serve, resolve conflicts or apologize. *How* it's done may vary according to a man's personality but *if* it's done is not even a question. Jesus said we are to make disciples, love our neighbors, and love God. Christ calls us to be active representatives for Him; we can't just wait for things to cross our paths or drop in our laps. Ladies, this of course also means that the man should be taking the lead role in your dating relationships (Prov. 18:22).

Intentionally Responsive *(Eph. 5:33)*

If you want to know how a woman deals with authority, you need to observe how she responds to anyone in authority over her and also how she responds to other men. Does she have a kind attitude or a sharp response? Is she respectful to men or does she belittle them? How does she treat the authorities in her life? Men, you need to think seriously about this characteristic in a woman because it is the essence of submission. We're not talking about whether she's introverted or extroverted. WARNING: Quiet or introverted personalities do not guarantee a submissive spirit. This is one of the most common mistakes men make. A woman's willingness to submit or respond to authority is demonstrated when she chooses to submit her opinions, decisions, and will to someone else **with a gracious attitude**. Whether it's with a girlfriend, a parent, co-worker, or potential husband, it's important to observe her *willingness* to not be in control regardless of her *capability* to be in control.

> **WARNING:** *Quiet or introverted personalities do not guarantee a submissive spirit.*

Teachability *(Luke 8:25)*

In Luke 8:25 Jesus asked the disciples, "Where is your faith?" He had just spent most of chapter 8 sharing wonderful parables and teachings. His last teaching was about the mustard seed. Jesus explained that though it was one of the smallest seeds it yielded one of the largest plants (up to 12 feet in height!). Then in verse 25 a fierce storm arose and the disciples became doubtful. They did not demonstrate teachability and it led to Jesus questioning their timidity. Would they ever learn? Later, in Luke 17:5, the disciples asked Jesus to increase their faith. They had finally become aware of their issue and were ready to hear what Christ had to say. Teachability is simply a characteristic that indicates a person's desire and ability to learn and continuously grow. It's the next step you take once you've embraced the idea of awareness. First, you know who you are, then you take steps to grow as you need to. It is critical that a potential mate be able to hear and respond to God's direction in every area of life. Teachability and awareness go hand in hand. Flexibility is another aspect of teachability and is one of the most important things in sustaining a healthy marriage. The opposite of flexibility is stubbornness or an unwillingness to move. It divides homes and destroys marriages. Stubbornness is rooted in self but flexibility is rooted in love for God and for others. God's Word clearly asks that we put others' interests (Phil. 2:3) over our own and love our neighbors as ourselves (Matt. 22:39). Is the person you're evaluating willing to change his or her opinion? Can that person learn from anyone and anything? Does that person always have to have his or her way or does that person understand how to choose battles wisely?

Humility before God *(Matt. 23:12; Phil. 2:5-8)*

Humility before God is demonstrated by how people live out their spiritual lives on a daily basis. The highpoints of Sunday or Wednesday services are not good reflections of a person's humility for God. You need opportunities to see that person in the mundane activities of life in order to observe the fruit from his or her relationship with Christ. Are they as passionate about pleasing Him as they are about achieving their own personal goals? Are they genuinely hurt when they disappoint Christ? Do they serve faithfully in Kingdom ministry? Are pride and arrogance trademarks of this person's character? Answering these questions can provide important insight into a person's spiritual life.

Humility before God, shown through a heart for God, is essential for any future spouse. Without it, you may find your life becoming as dry as the wilderness the Israelites wandered in for so many years because of their lack of humility. In Matthew 23:12, Jesus made it clear that if we focus on being exalted, He will make sure we are humbled. If Jesus sees humility as an important quality, then we should too.

Considering these traits, the significance of F.A.I.T.H. is evident when you're trying to recognize a potential mate. The point of these traits is not to have some legalistic checklist that you are using to disqualify people but to have some basic principles to identify in others that will help lay the foundation for a strong, healthy, dynamic marriage. Remember that before you decide if a potential mate demonstrates these qualities, take a look in the mirror. Of course we will have some areas we are stronger in and some areas that will always be challenging for us and this will also be true for the person we're evaluating. But the bottom line is we must remove the log out of our eye before we can address the speck in the eye of our brother or sister. Keep the F.A.I.T.H.!

Beyond Traits ... Looking beneath the surface

The more we've shared this F.A.I.T.H. principle the more we've come to realize how some people can fake these qualities to some extent. We have met many men and women who have mastered the art of performing these five qualities. They seem to possess many of these attributes but when we, or a potential mate, take a deeper look beneath the surface, a different picture emerges.

We call this the "lemon principle." This happens when what you see on the outside doesn't always give an accurate picture of what's going on inside and it can be dangerous. We call it the lemon principle because it's the same issue you may face when purchasing a used car. You need to know if what's under the hood matches the sparkling exterior. Truth be told, we are all used. But we don't have to be "lemons." Many newlyweds realize, after it's too late, that they didn't dig far enough beneath the surface and they find themselves feeling duped or deceived about whom they married.

Most of us would not buy a car solely based on how it looks, so why does that become so important when choosing the person with whom we will spend the rest of our lives? Where is the logic in that approach? If you're already in a relationship and you want to avoid getting a "lemon," consider this seven-point character inspection.

1. **Do you have a mechanic?** Genesis 2:24 says that when a man "leaves" his father and mother and joins to his wife, they become one flesh. The *mechanic* in our analogy here represents a covering. God's design is that the husband and wife "leave and cleave" (KJV) to each other. Ladies, you go from the covering of your parents (or spiritual parents) to the covering of your husband. Men, as the head of your household, you move from your spiritual covering and become your wife's covering. Does your potential mate have a spiritual covering? Who is assisting you and your potential mate with making major decisions?

2. **Do you know the history of the car?** When you buy a used car, you usually want to know the accidents the car has been in and any other "trouble areas" that may exist. Likewise, long before you walk down the aisle with a person, you need to know his or her history. This is not for judgment or disqualification, but it is vital to know some information about your potential mate's history. For example, it's important to know if he or she ever observed a successful marriage in their family history. Knowing someone's history can make the difference in how you approach your relationship and can clue you in to challenges you may face in the future. Keep in mind that to expect others to share their history requires that you be accepting and affirming as they reveal the scars that lie beneath the surface.

3. **Does the relationship suffer from the Armor All complex?** Have you ever walked into a used car dealership and been blinded by the shine of a car? All that Armor All is sometimes just an attempt to hide the imperfections that exist. The seller wants you to be so overwhelmed with the car's external attributes that you don't even ask the important questions. 1 Chronicles 28:9 declares, "And you, Solomon my son, obey the God of your father and serve him with a submissive attitude and a willing spirit, for the Lord examines all minds and understands every motive of one's thoughts. If you seek him, he will meet with you, but if you abandon him, he will reject you permanently." During the course of your relationship have you asked the important questions? Or have you been so "taken" with his/her external attributes that you're ooh-ing and aah-ing without noticing that black smoke is shooting out of the exhaust pipe? Be careful, even

the best applied Armor All washes off with the first rain.

4. **Does he/she have a reliable dipstick?** A mechanic uses a "dipstick" to determine the level of oil in a vehicle. The importance of oil in a car goes without saying—it preserves the life of the engine, the most important component inside a vehicle. In Matthew 12:34 Jesus said, "Offspring of vipers! How are you able to say anything good, since you are evil? For the mouth speaks from what fills the heart." Since the heart is the most important component in a person, the "dipstick" I'm referring to here is the tongue. In relationships, the tongue is the dipstick that will show you what's in another person's heart. James 3:2 says, "For we all stumble in many ways. If someone does not stumble in what he says, he is a perfect individual, able to control the entire body as well." What is coming out of your potential mate's mouth? By simply listening to a person talk, you can learn a great deal about who he/she is.

5. **Who has the keys?** In Inspection point 4, the statement was made that the heart was the most important component of a person. The heart is to us what an engine is to a car. Without the keys, however, that car will not go anywhere. Placing the key into the ignition, and turning it, starts the engine and gets the car ready to drive. Just as you would not give your car keys to just anyone (and thereby give them access to drive your car), you need to be sure of who holds the keys to your potential mate's heart. Proverbs 4:23 exhorts us to "Guard your heart with all vigilance, for from it are the sources of life." You need to know if your potential mate has given the keys to his or her heart to anyone

else. Is he or she still talking with a previous "special" someone from a past relationship? If you don't know who has the keys, you may walk out of your front door one day and discover that the car in your driveway is gone.

6. **Check your speed: how fast are you going?** Philippians 4:6 declares, "Do not be anxious about anything. Instead, in every situation, through prayer and petition with thanksgiving, tell your requests to God." How fast are you moving in your relationship? Are you prayerfully moving toward marriage? While it is important to make sure you do all that you can to determine if this is the right mate for you, this process should not drag on for years and years. You must remember that there are two hearts involved in this process. A person's heart was not designed to be "led on" for years and years or bonded to another without a commitment being made. Can we tell you how long the courtship or dating process should take? No. But we are saying that both of you should **honestly** communicate clearly to each other your expectations so that hearts are not broken in the process. If you are too tough to be honest about your feelings, it will be impossible for the other person to make an accurate assessment of the emotional and spiritual temperature of the relationship. If you share your feelings and they are disregarded, this may be another exit sign.

7. **Are the rims more valuable than the rest of the car?** (Matt. 6:19-21) If you see a car that has accessories that are more valuable than the car itself, you may be looking at a lemon. Spending too much money on enhancements like speakers, rims,

radio systems, etc. don't make much sense if the same investment hasn't been made on the "unseen" aspects of the car such as the engine, transmission, or the air conditioning. Why is this question important to consider? Money! Money! Money! This is one way to determine how your potential mate spends money. While financial status is not critical to a successful marriage, financial values are. A fight over money (how it's spent and the lack of it) is one of the top five reasons for divorces today. Does he or she value external things more than internal things? A nice new suit or beautiful new dress is meaningless if there is no beauty or character underneath.

Okay, another checklist and more information. So what's a woman to do when a man has expressed interest? What is a man's next step once he becomes interested? Reread this chapter (slowly) and rely on F.A.I.T.H. to help you observe your potential mate. Most importantly, relax and let God speak to your heart. If you listen and obey, He will never lead you astray.

our story: *"he said, she said"*

his side of the story

During early 2000, I began observing a young lady in our church. She was serving in our youth ministry as the Youth Worship Leader and on the team of Senior High teachers. She devoted herself to ministry. When she was not serving in either of those two categories, she was serving in the young adult choir at our church. Somehow it seemed as if she was always in my presence. She knew nothing about me observing her, but I was. I was evaluating her. I was not simply looking for a girlfriend; I was looking for a life partner. In early 1999, I and some of my friends from seminary had decided to pray for our mates every week. We were each asking God to send us a woman who loved God and exhibited high character. So for me, the question was not only a matter of her being attractive—which she happened to be – but a matter of character. I needed to know if she had the qualities necessary to build a lasting family, a healthy relationship, and a God-honoring future, no matter what that future held. I had to ask some questions: (1) Was she flexible? (2) Was she aware? (3) Was she intentionally submissive? (4) Was she teachable? (5) Did she have a humility before God? These qualities were of paramount importance because they indicate whether someone will be a healthy mate, and they were also the qualities Jesus Himself looked for in the disciples He selected to change the world. *In Matthew 4, Jesus found* *disciples who were <u>faithful and flexible</u>; they dropped what they were doing to follow him. He found men who were <u>aware</u>; they knew they had encountered the one John the Baptist had preached about. They were also <u>submissive and teachable</u>, which was mandatory in order to "follow Him" as He commanded.*

To continue my information gathering, I observed her as she interacted with her friends. Did she have more guy friends than girlfriends? Who were her mentors? What was the quality of the girls she hung out with? All these questions were important to me, and so I simply observed her to see whether I could get answers to these questions without engaging her heart. In order to do this, I had to pray and trust God to allow our paths to cross over the course of the next several months. I knew that it would have been very difficult to seek the answers to these questions objectively if I was falling in love with her at the same time as I was observing her. The worst thing I could have done was to engage her heart or get her (or my) emotions involved. In order to prevent that from happening and avoid another broken heart, I tried my best to pursue observing her without her knowing it.

One problem I had early on was that all the stories I heard of her were glowing. It was all great, but because I knew she was a human being, I knew she had to have some issues. My next pursuit then was to identify some enemies. I wanted to find some people who had worked with her and did not like her for one reason or the other. I needed to know what those reasons were and how she handled confrontation. Again, my desire was to try to discern her heart and character. What better way to identify potential traits than to ask people who struggled working with her. Now don't get me wrong. I was not looking for angry, self-absorbed individuals who simply wanted to "dump" on me about her. I was looking for patterns in behavior to expose cracks in her character, because the Word of God states that the most important thing in life is our name or our reputation (Prov. 22:1). From her enemies I found out that she was committed to excellence, did not tolerate mediocrity, was articulate, talked a little too much, and had a quick tongue. That's what her enemies said. I took note and began examining those traits to see if they were true.

I must say that the thing I liked the most about her was that she was not looking for a mate; she was simply serving God and trying to have as much fun as she could. Actually, I later learned that Jada and her friends really thought that she would be the last of her friends to get married. That was attractive. She was a saint who was serving God, and she was attractive and had a tender heart for Him. I thought, WOW!

After I was about three quarters of the way through my observing process, I

> *I was looking for patterns in behavior to expose cracks in her character, because the Word of God states that the most important thing in life is our name or our reputation.*

asked a friend of mine, the Youth Pastor of our church at the time, about her service as a volunteer in the Youth Ministry. He had only great things to say about her. He confirmed many of my observations and answered some questions directly for me. However, he also told Jada (prematurely) that I liked her and so I had to clarify my intentions quicker than I had planned. The last thing I wanted was for her to wonder (dream) about some guy whom she "heard" liked her. I had learned the hard way (chapter 1) how easily a woman's emotions can become engaged.

Because Jada was informed by our Youth Pastor, the observation period had to end. I now had to clarify how this relationship would be different, and I had to begin protecting her heart by communicating a clear vision of the direction of the relationship. One day our mutual friend brought her over to the office and then I asked her if she minded giving me her phone number. She gave me her number and I called about two weeks later. I spent those weeks in prayer seeking God and asking him to lead and direct the relationship. Then I made the call and invited Jada to dinner. I had two reasons for dinner. First, I needed to explain the situation that our friend had placed us in, and second, I needed to lay out a plan for our relationship. The following nine steps were used as a roadmap to give her direction and provide accountability and guidance for me (at this point steps 1-4 were already complete).

1. Be Under a Covering (i was under the covering of my father and two other mentors)

2. Identify Timeless Traits: What makes a healthy marriage? Is the young lady Faithful, Aware, Intentionally submissive, Teachable, and demonstrating Humility before God? (This was already done.)

3. Observation: I looked and asked about these five qualities. (This was already done.)

4. Make Contact: A conversation initiated by me to give clear direction (Engage Her Heart)

5. Enaging the Heart (this happened when I asked Jada to dinner); Observation by Jada immediately followed

6. Courtship

7. Engagement

8. Marriage

9. Continue to meet with a mentor couple

At dinner we had a blast. Initially, it was a little awkward; I had a list of questions that I asked her, based on the timeless traits mentioned above. It was important to discern what she valued as an individual and as a Christian, but what was supposed to be a two hour-dinner ended up being a five-hour conversation. She was simply terrific. Many of my questions were answered and many of my concerns were taken care of. At dinner, however, my primary goal was to clarify my intentions for the relationship. I had to set direction and lay the foundation upon which the relationship would rest. So I did the following six things: (1) I shared my philosophy on dating, courting, and marriage, (2) I apologized for not sharing my interest in her myself, (3) I shared that I had the opportunity to observe her but that I realized that she needed to observe me, (4) I shared with her that she could have the time she needed, but that it would not be wise for that time frame to be indefinite and that we could have check-in points, (5) I shared my commitment to her as a woman of God and as a sister in Christ, and (6) I committed my desire to ensure that she would grow closer to God because of this relationship and that I would do my best to ensure that she was a better person because God allowed our paths to cross.

The Trip to Israel

The relationship continued for weeks, and we got to know each other better. We went out on dates with other couples, we did ministry together, I met her friends, she met my friends, and we got to ask the hard questions of each other's friends, and we heard fascinating anecdotes of each other's past. We decided that the relationship was progressing well and so we had to make a decision as to whether we would enter a courtship period. As a part of my seminary training I had the opportunity to go to Israel. It was then that we decided that we would fast one day a week while we were apart for three weeks to discern if this was God's will for us. We concluded that at the end of the three weeks in Israel we would decide whether or not we would become engaged. During this time we sought counsel, prayed, and read two books: <u>Saving Your Marriage before It Starts</u>, by Dr.

Les Parrott III and Dr. Leslie Parrott and <u>The Triumphant Marriage</u>, by Dr. Neil Clark Warren. Our goal was to understand better what marriage was really all about and to begin evaluating how we felt about each other and whether we were each ready for a lifetime commitment.

When I returned from Israel, it was clear to me that she was definitely the one for me. But I wondered what she was thinking. Would she feel the same way I felt? She picked me up at the airport and we talked. She felt that God had been leading her in the same way. We both were overwhelmed with emotion by what we believed God was telling us. It was on that day that we decided that we would be married. We entered the courtship phase. I told Jada that she did not have to worry about whether I would change my mind. I would not. I was making a commitment to God and to her. It was as good as if we were married. I was that confident in God and in who she was becoming as a woman of God.

> *I told Jada that she did not have to worry about whether I would change my mind. I would not. I was making a commitment to God and to her.*

The Permission

Once we decided to be married, I knew I had to talk to her

father, her covering at the time. I set up a time to meet with him and let him know I wanted his permission to ask for his daughter's hand in marriage. We had an interesting and challenging conversation. Of course her father wanted to know all about me and my plans for his daughter. He wanted to make sure I wasn't flaky or lazy. Mr. Cobon asked about my family and listened to my words to assess my character. He did his job in protecting his daughter and making sure that she would be given only to a man who honored God and could protect and provide for her. It was tough – as it should be – but in the end Jada's father honored my request and granted me permission to propose.

The Engagement

I had always told Jada that from the moment we entered into a courtship, I could ask her to marry me at any time. Confident in her God, my character, and my leadership, she actually bought her wedding dress and began making plans because I had given her my word. I had not even bought her engagement ring yet but she could move forward with necessary plans because we both knew how committed we were to God, to each other, and to a life together.

The day finally came. I bought the ring and it was time to propose. I was nervous and scared, and I wondered if this was the right choice. Confident in God's Word and in Jada's character, I knew life together with her would be better than life alone. So I had two good friends assist me in creating the ambiance for the proposal. The night was set with dozens of roses, a violin playing her favorite song, and a full moon. It was perfect. I proposed to her in her parent's backyard while her dad was inside without a clue as to what was going on. I felt pretty smooth.

We walked in to share the news with her dad, and to our surprise the doorbell rang. It was two of her best friends who coincidentally came over to visit. She was shocked, and I was shocked. It was not planned, and I could not take credit for it. They were all elated, and we all celebrated together.

The Wedding

It took place at the First Baptist Church, Dallas, which is known for its history and architecture. My mentor, pastor, and spiritual father officiated the wedding. Our families were all present and some of our best friends were standing with us. We wanted to prepare for life together, not just a wedding. As soon as I asked Jada to marry me, I asked her to read a book called, Inviting God to Your Wedding, by Martha Williamson. It helps brides-to-be and grooms-to-be keep the right focus as they plan their nuptials. We committed early on to making sure that our wedding day would be distinctively biblical, and would celebrate God and His plan for salvation and sanctification. Our wedding was designed to model this reality of the return of Christ for his bride. We wanted a worship service, not just a wedding. Our dream wedding included an evangelistic appeal, not just an entertaining attraction. We planned it based on Revelation 19:7 which says, "Let us rejoice and exalt and give him glory, because the wedding celebration of the Lamb has come, and his bride has made herself ready. "

In this passage, the bride (the church) is supposed to ready herself for the Groom (Christ) when He returns. The principle of a man taking the initiative and "finding" his wife is also seen in the verse. It perfectly captures the essence of our relationship and the relationship between Christ and His bride. This backdrop also created a great opportunity to present the gospel of Jesus Christ.

Planning for a Lifetime Together

One of the most powerful things any human being can have is a picture of the future. What will our marriage look like? What are our values? What is it that we are asking God to do in us and then through us? What are we involved in that will demand us staying on our knees as a couple and as a family? What are we doing that is bigger than ourselves and that will make a difference in this world? What legacy will we leave for our family for generations to come?

During our courtship these questions guided our discussions and we created a manifesto of sorts that would be used to give direction to our future family. It was a plan that would keep us from drifting; it was our hope that it would keep us focused and prevent us from allowing the world to determine our priorities. To achieve our vision and to ensure that we continually grow, Jada and I had annual goals in each of the following seven categories:

Emotional: To be balanced emotionally means that you do not overreact or underreact in the midst of a crisis or when faced with a difficult situation. It also means not withholding or internalizing your emotions and not verbally responding in disgust or anger.

Physical: To be balanced physically means that you understand that you are fearfully and wonderfully made. You recognize that your body is the temple of the Holy Spirit and you take care of it by eating well, exercising consistently, getting enough sleep, and getting regular physical checkups.

Financial: To be balanced financially means that you are living below your means, not above them. You have a financial plan and follow the "give, save, spend" model of stewardship.

Spiritual: To be balanced spiritually means that you are consistently "showing off" God's glory with your life by living out the fruit of the Spirit in your relationships, growing, reaching out in evangelism, being connected to a small group of Christians, and being a good steward with the gifts and resources that God has given you.

Professional: To be balanced professionally means that you know what you do best and are committed to developing those God-given talents to their fullest potential.

Personal: To be balanced personally means you ask and answer these questions: Who are you becoming in light of God's design for a man or woman? Whose image of manhood and womanhood are you following? What is your reputation? As a man, are you rejecting passivity, accepting responsibility, and loving sacrificially? As a woman, do you support and respect those in authority over you, empower and nurture those you come in contact with, relate to others with authentic connection, value the principle of a spiritual covering, and enhance the lives of others with your internal beauty?

Relational: To be balanced relationally means that you possess healthy same-sex relationships and that there are one, two, or three people that you are willing to love sacrificially and are engaging in battle for their souls. It also means that when interacting with the opposite sex I (Conway) will follow 1 Timothy 5:2, "and [treat] younger women as sisters—with complete purity."

For each of the previous seven areas we each have three or four goals that we try to accomplish each year.

Today, we are still trusting God and trying our best to stay balanced in these areas. Although we are far from perfect, we have seen over and over again that honoring God in our relationship has been a significant foundation on which to build a healthy marriage.

her side of the story

In March of 2000 I took a trip to New York City to visit Columbia University. I had decided to get an M.B.A. degree, and I wanted to get into a top school and Columbia was my last chance. I had taken the right test, filled out the right applications, and was focused on pursuing my degree. At that time I had been serving in the youth ministry at my church for about two years. I was very involved serving as a core team leader, teacher for the twelfth-grade Bible class and worship leader for the youth praise team. It was a very fulfilling and challenging time for me. The Lord was stretching me and I was so excited to be immersed in ministry, but I was ready for a change of scenery so I decided to pursue graduate school. While at Columbia University I got to see the campus, meet with an advisor, and imagine my life in New York. I just knew it would be awesome. I figured that was one of the benefits of being single—having the freedom to move and change my life whenever I wanted.

The next month, in April, I received a letter from Columbia. I quickly read through the traditional introductory language, "…it was a pleasure meeting with you…you seem to be a strong candidate… however…" When I read "however" my eyes lingered there and my heart sunk. I knew what was next. The letter said that I was being placed on a waiting list and would have priority in applying *next year*. I remember how defeated I felt. It was like I wasn't smart enough, and my plans were failing. I asked God why He couldn't just let me get into school and move to New York. I sulked for the next several weeks.

About four weeks later, during early May, I was at church on a Wednesday night discussing some ministry issues with our Youth Pastor. During our conversation he abruptly interrupted. "Guess who likes you?" I groaned inside. A relationship was the farthest thing from my mind and I couldn't think of anyone that I might be interested in that he would even know, but I played along.

"Who?" I asked. His face lit up with excitement. "Conway Edwards!" he said.

"Who?" I asked again. I was still puzzled.

I had never heard that name before and I thought I knew everybody at church. He went on to give me a passionate but awkward sales pitch about this Conway Edwards. He quickly told me how great Conway was. He told me that he was a seminarian, that he was on staff at the church and that he planned to move to Jamaica some day to do full-time ministry. I was taken aback. Nothing in that description enticed me. After a couple of experiences I had sworn off seminarians because I assumed they were all stuffy, boring, and sheltered. I knew I needed someone who was fun loving, appreciated a free spirit, and lived a pretty laid-back life. That didn't describe any seminary students I knew. In addition to that, I certainly wasn't excited by a life of full-time ministry, especially in another country! That was a strange resume but it was enough for me to realize that whoever this guy was, he wasn't for me.

The next Sunday I remember realizing who Conway was when I saw him at church for the first time. "How strange," I thought.

This guy has been at the church for five years and this is the first time I even knew who he was. I tried to wave at him, confident that he would wave back since he was interested in me, but he didn't respond. I lingered around a little to see if he would walk over and talk to me. After all, *he* liked *me*. But he didn't acknowledge me. He just kept socializing. I was a little irritated. My pride had gotten the best of me. "Oh well," I thought. "It doesn't matter anyway."

A couple of weeks passed and I was at church doing some more ministry work with my Youth Pastor. He said, "Let's walk to the main building because this copier isn't working." I blindly followed him, and we wound up in Conway's cubicle. I'm sure I had the deer-in-the-headlights look. I hated this awkward feeling. I felt like a schoolgirl playing silly games. I was never big on matchmaking and now I had become a victim. After standing at Conway's desk for seconds of silence that seemed like eternity, my Youth Pastor "mysteriously" had to leave and go do something. That left Conway and me alone making uncomfortable small talk. Finally, Conway said, "You know, I think you and I need to talk." I assumed he was alluding to the fact that I knew about his interest in me. He then said, "May I have your phone number so we can talk?" I proceeded to give him my number, and I left there as soon as I could.

One day went by and I received no phone call. Several days went by and still no phone call. One week passed and I began to wonder if Conway would ever call. I wasn't even sure why I cared but for some reason I was actually anticipating hearing from him. Finally, after two weeks, Conway called at work one day. It was a conversation I'll never forget. This person I didn't know began asking me some pretty personal questions right away. He wanted to know what I loved about ministry, who my close friends were, and what women at the church I admired. I answered all of his questions and he seemed satisfied with my answers. He then apologized for how I found out about his interest in me and suggested that we get together to discuss the "confusion" that may have resulted. He suggested the Cheesecake Factory! I was so thrilled that a sheltered seminarian knew of a fun place to eat. In that one conversation Conway set himself apart from any man I had ever met. He was most interested in who I was as a person, my ministry, and the people who influenced me. I was so refreshed and encouraged that if he and I had never spoken again I would have still been better for the conversation alone. We set the "dinner discussion" for later in the week and said good-bye.

> *He said he had learned the hard way how precious a woman's heart was and he wanted to do everything he could to protect mine.*

The night of our "discussion" had finally arrived. I met Conway at the Cheesecake Factory at six that evening. His plan was to tell me that this was all a misunderstanding and that we should probably just go our separate ways. My plan was to "let him down easy." I was going to let him know that I appreciated his interest but this probably wouldn't work out. After all, I wasn't remotely interested in a relationship.

Five hours later, at the request of the restaurant staff, we left our table to finish talking outside. Conway had shared that although he hadn't planned to tell me he was interested until much later, he believed that God had sovereignly allowed our paths to cross. He said God allowed us to meet for one of three reasons: (1) to be friends for life, (2) to be friends for a season, or (3) to be married. I thought to myself, did he just say *married*? Conway continued to explain his philosophy of relationships and marriage. He told me that he didn't believe in lengthy, drawn-out relationships and that "should I accept this mission" he would try his best to guard my heart. He said he had learned the hard way how precious a woman's heart was and he wanted to do everything he could to protect mine.

Conway had dominated most of the conversation with prepared questions about me, my likes and dislikes, my family and my values. He was trying to analyze me but I refused to be figured out. We played conversational chess. Both of us tried to ask questions that would provide insight about the other. I was absolutely impressed by his confidence and boldness as a Christian man as well as the sharpness of his mind. As our talk came to an end in the parking lot, Conway suggested that we not talk for the next week but spend that time praying about what direction God might give us. I agreed and we reluctantly parted ways. We were both surprised by how easily the conversation had flowed. As I drove home that night, I had to wonder if God was up to something.

Over the next week I received two very sweet cards from Conway thanking me for the evening we shared and reminding me that he was praying for me. Technically he had cheated and broken our agreement not to talk for a week. I was enamored. I remember telling my mom all about our night and showing her the two cards. She was excited for me as moms always are.

The week came to an end and Conway and I talked about what would become of our encounter. It didn't take long for us to both agree that God was definitely giving us the green light to move forward. Conway then laid out the next step in his "plan." It all seemed so formal. But the casual approach (based on past relationships) hadn't worked at all so I was open to how he wanted to proceed. He said that he wanted to give me some time to observe him and talk to his friends so I could make my own judgments. It was then that I found out Conway had been observing me, and a couple of other young ladies, for almost a year. I was shocked. He told me that he would like to set a time when we would decide if the relationship was headed for marriage. It all happened pretty fast. I couldn't believe I was contemplating marrying someone I had known less than two months. I didn't think it was possible to come to such a serious decision in such a short time. Then the Lord spoke to my heart. He reminded me that all of my hesitancy was based on shallow desires and preferences, not on His principles. So I prayed about it and decided to go along with the "plan."

Conway was taking a trip to Israel in the next few weeks. He would be gone for about three weeks. I specifically remember that his return date was June 12 so that would be the date we would decide whether to move forward toward marriage. Conway and I talked enough while he was in Israel to rack up a good-sized phone bill. We started to discuss some pretty deep issues about what we wanted out of life and how we viewed marriage. Conway seriously discussed the possibility of living in Jamaica and for some reason I felt an overwhelming ease about it. It wasn't anything like I had imagined it would be but his confidence—which was rooted in Christ—about our relationship made me comfortable in doing whatever he felt was best. We had decided to purchase journals before he left for Israel and I was writing in mine everyday. I was counting the days until his return.

The day Conway came home I went to the airport to pick him up. It was a tense morning. I already knew what God was confirming in my heart, and I was pretty sure he felt the same way. I saw him and we engaged in small talk for a while and got in the car to head home. After about five minutes of driving he said, "Pull the car over." I pulled over and he looked me directly in my eyes and said, "I am certain that you are to be my wife." All I could say was "Ok. I'm ready to move forward." My heart was beating so fast and I couldn't believe what was happening. He seemed so calm and we had just made a major life decision! We drove home chatting about everything in the world as if it was the most normal day of our lives.

From that point on, I knew that Conway could propose at any moment, so I figured it might be a good idea to let my dad know how serious this was. A few days later I told my dad that Conway would be coming over for dinner to have a discussion with him. My dad had that wrinkled brow when he said "About what?" I said, "Our relationship." I'm sure he was in denial and that was the last thing he wanted to hear from his oldest daughter, so all I got from my dad was a grunt and he mumbled, "Okay. Whatever." We arranged for

Conway to come over for dinner sometime in the last week of June. My dad didn't make it easy but Conway cornered him while he was outside in the backyard to ask him for my hand in marriage. When they emerged from their outside chat, Conway looked calm but he gave me the signal that everything had gone well. That was a miracle in itself! My dad wasn't an easy "sell," but Conway's character and my trust in him sealed the deal.

Our relationship progressed and we worked hard to maintain healthy boundaries and keep our emotions in check. Of course it was difficult but we constantly sought the Lord on how He would guide our relationship. We read marriage preparation books and went through premarital counseling. I remember countless conversations wrestling with core issues in our relationship. We discussed all our plans and desires with the Lord, and Conway brought amazing clarity to the courtship. During July and August we spent intentional time together learning about each other's lives. I got to see Conway's seminary life and meet several of his friends and ask their opinions on him. They all had great things to say. They loved his passion and enthusiasm and said he truly had a heart for God. I even got to hear about his weaknesses from a couple of very honest friends whom he trusted deeply. In August Conway and I headed to Jamaica to meet his family. I was nervous to be meeting my future in-laws but they welcomed me with open arms. I felt even stronger about our future after seeing the godly foundation his parents had laid, and the Lord was already preparing my heart for living in Jamaica one day.

By September, although Conway had not officially proposed, I began looking for a wedding dress and taking care of big wedding details. Because we considered ourselves engaged, we had already set our wedding date. After a lot of searching I found a beautiful church and a dress that fit me and my personality just perfectly.

My friends and family were quite skeptical about this whirlwind relationship. They couldn't believe that I had just met Conway less than five months earlier, that he was a student who wanted to pursue ministry in a third world country, and I was making wedding plans without a ring on my finger. It just wasn't the way things were supposed to go. I told them repeatedly that if a piece of jewelry on my hand was more valuable than Conway's promise to marry me (his word), we were in big trouble. At times I felt very alone but I had every confidence that this was the right move for me. That time prepared me to be able to follow his leadership even when others (including my family) didn't agree. I tried to explain to them how God had changed so many of my insignificant preferences and had shown me the important principles that build a lasting marriage.

In October, with a full moon shining bright, my favorite hymn being played by a violin, dozens of red roses and of course the element of surprise, Conway proposed. I accepted and we were official.

We were married in March 2001, less than one year after I met him and it continues to be an exciting and challenging ride. After salvation of course, marrying Conway was the best decision I have made in my life.

Concluding Thoughts (your stories)

After reading our story, a lot of thoughts may be running through your head. Ladies, you might be asking the Lord if a man is ever going to pursue you. Men, you might be asking Him if there is a woman out there for you or if you are really ready for such a commitment? We can't encourage you enough that God is very clear that marriage is something that is to be accomplished in His own timing and in His way. We want you to know that God loves you, cherishes you, and wants you to thrive in your everyday life. He also desires to use you for His purposes, and time is of the essence. Am I (Conway) saying that you should put your feelings on the back burner and deny them? No,

> *Marriage is not a guarantee of happiness or joy; as Jada and I have realized, it is hard work.*

by all means, pray that God will send the individual in His timing and His way. But until that time, we want to challenge and encourage you to become involved in His work and in doing what pleases Him. Perhaps marriage is not in your immediate future. It may not be in your future at all. So if you delay taking risks for God and maximizing your gifts and resources for His glory, your delay is in vain. God wants us to live for Him regardless of what we may be waiting on to make life complete.

Being single is not an excuse to feel sorry for yourself, or to feel as if you are not good enough to be married. The couples you see at church, on your job, or leisurely walking by the lake constantly deal with some very heavy issues. As you have read in this book, the issues you carry do not disappear when love finds you. Marriage is not a guarantee of happiness or joy; as Jada and I have realized, it is hard work.

So continue to hope and dream, but also begin to get involved (or further involved) in the plans that God has for you and in His work through a local church. In this game of life there is always work for God's team. Remember, "The harvest is plentiful but the workers are few" (Matt. 9:37). It is our prayer that you will get off the sidelines, stop being a spectator, and get in the game. If you are one of those single Christians who stand on the wall at the club and/or surf the net hoping for that chance to interact with the opposite sex, let it go! Trust God to bring your mate, and in the meantime be busy serving Him.

As you read in our story, although each of us wanted to be married some day, we made the decision as singles, to allow God to have control in that area of our lives, and to serve faithfully until His perfect will became evident in our lives.

take the lead

8

One of our favorite movies is *Take the Lead*, directed by Liz Friedlander. Antonio Banderas portrays Pierre Dulaine, the real-life dance coach who tries to make a difference in the inner-city schools of New York. In his spare time, Pierre began a dance class for children who would normally not have the opportunity to learn it.

One of the aspects we liked most about the movie was how ballroom dancing was used as a great illustration of how a man is supposed to lead. He must lead in a way that's graceful, yet provides certainty and security and the woman must be willing to follow him. The underlining principle in the movie was that if a man learns how to touch a woman with respect (through classical dance), then he is more likely to respect women in general. This is also true for women. If a woman knows how it feels to be touched with respect, and led with grace, she might not let a guy treat her any kind of way when it comes to relationships.

Men, our prayer is that you will lead courageously, graciously and embrace the incredible role that God has created for you. Women, our prayer is that you will expect good leadership and allow yourselves to respond well to it.

Our hope in writing this book is that men and women will be encouraged in their singleness and open to consider another view on dating, love and relationships. It is our prayer that something in this book will challenge every reader, whether single or married, to consider their present philosophy of dating and relationships and evaluate it in light of the word of God. In no way do we desire for this to be a legalistic manuscript, but rather a guide that will help facilitate healthy, God-honoring relationships.

So may you be consumed with God and His desires for your life. And while you do so, may He give you the desires of your heart.

frequently asked questions

Q1: *There's a guy who sits near me at church. We exchange friendly conversation from time to time during church and singles events. I would like to converse with him more outside of these brief encounters just to get to know him better. If a woman is not to initiate interaction with a man, what options do I have in this situation?*

A1: You're right. It's usually not wise for a woman to initiate interaction with a man she's interested in. We would suggest that you pray about it. Ask God to reveal His will to both of you and until He does, ask Him to help you control your emotions and desires for this man (no matter how trivial they may seem now). A godly man should understand God's order and will initiate if led to do so. Remember, men will go after what they want *when* they are ready. Philippians 4: 6-7 tells us, "Do not be anxious about anything. Instead, in every situation, through prayer and petition with thanksgiving, tell your requests to God. And the peace of God that surpasses all understanding will guard your hearts and minds in Christ Jesus."

123

Q2: How will a man know whether the woman he is interested in is interested in him? From what I understand, observation is a part of the process. But what if I spend two or three months observing, never really engaging her in any conversation, and it turns out she doesn't want to pursue anything with me? Should I consider that wasted time?

A2: Proverbs 3: 5-6 tells us to "Trust in the Lord with all your heart, and do not rely on your own understanding.

Acknowledge him in all your ways, and he will make your paths straight." Based on these verses, we would say: (1) do not rely on your own judgment alone, (2) ask God for guidance, (3) consider finding out more about her from trustworthy sources (e.g., a mutual friend or someone who knows her but won't inform her that you have inquired about her), (4) consider talking with her directly to get an indication of her initial reaction to you (merely talking to a woman is not "engaging her heart." It's what you say and how you say it that can cause her heart to be engaged.), and (5) remember that if your motives and intentions are pure, there is no such thing as wasted time. Even if a woman you observe is not interested in you, you will still benefit from practicing this selfless principle and trying your best to honor God in the process.

Q3: Is it wrong for a woman to propose?

A3: 1 Corinthians 14:40 reads, "And do everything in a decent and orderly manner." Proverbs 18:22 reads, "The one who finds a wife finds what is enjoyable, and receives a pleasurable gift from the Lord." It is very important that you remember to wait on God. In addition, a woman proposing to a man is the clearest sign of initiation there is! Do you really want to marry a man who didn't ask you to be His wife? You are a precious, special gift for the man who has the boldness and confidence in Christ to initiate the engagement process with you. One of the dangers of a woman proposing to a man is that it automatically reverses the roles of the man and woman involved and this issue is likely to cross over into marriage.

Q4: How does a single person protect his or her heart?

A4: Keep in mind that there are both verbal and nonverbal forms of engaging the heart. Verbal forms include: having deep discussions where emotions, vulnerabilities, and innermost feelings are shared or revealed, when flirtatious words or thoughts are expressed and when sexual or physical desires are expressed. Nonverbal forms include extended eye contact, winking, physical touch such as rubbing, massages, and hugging. Of course more obvious nonverbal forms are kissing and being physically intimate. You can protect your heart by being aware of your own emotions when engaging in these and other verbal and nonverbal behaviors. Of course, these behaviors above are not all inclusive. Ask God to sharpen your self-awareness so that you are better able to discern what behaviors can trigger or engage your heart. Being honest with yourself and setting appropriate boundaries is critical to successfully protecting your heart.

Q5: Christian dating seems too difficult. I've pretty much chosen not to date at all. I wish we could just have friends of the opposite sex to hang out with from time to time, but I know (from experience) that doesn't work. What's a girl to do?

A5: Galatians 6: 6-9 tells us, "So we must not grow weary in doing good, for in due time we will reap, if we do not give up." Please stay encouraged and remember that Christian dating/ courtship does require discipline just like the Christian walk itself. One of Satan's biggest traps is to deceive us into thinking that doing anything God's way is either too difficult, impossible, or doesn't consider our best interest. While Christian dating is not always easy, it is undoubtedly the most rewarding. Let me tell you why: (1) <u>God is at the center of our focus.</u> Society tells us to focus on ourselves, our interests, and how the person we are dating can meet our needs. (2) We learn some key disciplines that will equip us to be godly husbands and wives. (3) We assist each other in our Christian walk instead of causing each other to stumble in their walk. When a man and woman are operating in true Christian dating/courtship they value their relationship as brother and sister in Christ. This allows them to inspire and encourage each other to grow in their walk as Christians. This is the kind of relationship that can be beneficial to both people

126

involved, even if it doesn't end in marriage. (4) We show God that we believe and have faith in Him. It's amazing how singles trust God with all areas of their lives except in the area of dating and courtship. How much do we really love God? Do we love Him enough to give ourselves completely to Him? First Thessalonians 4:3 tells us that sexual purity is God's purpose and will for us. For a single person, that is the ultimate act of faith.

Q6: Why does it seem that many Christian men prefer not to court the Christian ladies in their own church?

A6: A lot of factors contribute to this issue. There is always an added set of pressures for a man to both approach and court a woman who attends his church. Some men feel uncomfortable because they feel that every move they make is being watched and that they may be perceived as not having a true spiritual focus or motive. Other men fear the potential consequences that may result from being rejected in their church environment. For example, if a man approaches a woman at a mall and gets rejected, he most likely will never see her again. However, if a man gets rejected at his own church he will be reminded of it every Sunday when he sees her. Consider the pressure of being rejected by one woman only to try again by approaching another woman, and unfortunately being rejected again. If a man is not careful with his judgment, he could very easily become labeled as a womanizer, a player, or just someone who is not focused on true fellowship. There are some men who are intimidated or hesitant to approach a woman who is consistently "chatting with her girls" before and after church services. This setting only intensifies the "I don't want to be perceived as a Mack-daddy" syndrome. Don't misinterpret this, a woman should not deliberately disassociate herself from fellowship with her girlfriends hoping that a man will approach her. The godly man God has for you will find a way to approach you no matter what the barriers are. Other men don't feel comfortable courting a woman who attends his own church because it creates a more intense level of accountability. Some women may be wondering, "How does this prevent a man from approaching me?" Well, think about it. A man who is not serious in his walk with the Lord might not feel totally comfortable approaching a woman he knows is very serious about her walk with the Lord (based on having observed her demonstrate such traits in her service and interactions at church).

Q7: I need help with the concept of "Christian Dating." I have found many Christian men are just as superficial as non-Christian men. It seems they want to put you through all types of tests before they even attempt to engage your mind, much less your heart. By the time I am at the point where a man wants to engage my heart, I'm wiped out. I have no more to give. This is why I don't date. It is a lot to think of another person and try your best to relate to him only to realize he was trying to see if you would pass some test.

A7: Both single men and women in churches around the country often have this perception about each other. Remember, just because a man goes to church does not mean he is living by the Word of God. In every church there is a broad spectrum of people. Some regular church goers aren't even Christians while some walk closely with God and have given Him control over every aspect of their lives. This is why it is so important to observe people and their interactions at church. You'd be surprised at how much you can learn about a person and his or her level of spiritual focus just by watching that person. It is also important to make sure you represent what it is that you want to attract. Since you aren't dating right now, use this time to work on yourself, and in God's timing He'll send the right man to you. Please don't be discouraged. It is admirable of you to have allowed yourself to trust Christian dating instead of worldly dating. But while you are waiting, please understand that not all Christian men are superficial. It only takes meeting that one real man of God for your life to be changed and blessed with a godly marriage. So don't allow your past experiences with the wrong men to distort what you know about God and what He can do for you. Remember, "I am able to do all things through the one who strengthens me" (Phil. 4:13).

Q8: Why does God allow us to have urges that we can't control (in other words, natural strong desires) and can't do anything about it while single? I've prayed those urges away, but I still get them often. I monitor who I'm around, what I watch, and

what I listen to, and stay in the Word and in church, and in prayer.

A8: 1 Thessalonians 4:1-8 argues that purity is God's purpose and will for us as singles. 1 Corinthians 6:13-20 tells us that (1) we are to flee fornication, (2) we are not our own, and (3) we were bought with a price. The urges we have were never intended to be acted on in our single life. They are meant to be used only in the context of marriage. Satan wants us to believe that we can't control the urges we have. However, the fact that God commands us not to act on them also confirms that we do have the power to control them. We know this because God never gives us a command without giving us the strength or a way to follow it. Has a man really truly ever controlled his urges? Yes. One of the best illustrations of this can be found in the Book of Job. In Job 1:8, God describes Job as a blameless and upright man. Later in 31:1, Job reveals that he made a covenant with his eyes not to look lustfully at a girl. You see Job himself was just a man. But he made a covenant not to allow lust to rule his life. We too have the power within us through the Holy Spirit to control urges. But it begins with taking and maintaining the following steps: (1) consistently ask God for help to control the urges *(We ask God for everything else. Why not ask Him to remove the spirit of sexual immorality from us? Some of us allow the guilt from past failures to interfere with our comfort level of asking God for help in this matter.)*, (2) make a promise to God to remain sexually pure at all costs *(In Luke 9:23 Jesus said, "If anyone wants to become my follower, he must deny himself, take up his cross daily, and follow me." As singles, to follow Jesus it will cost you your sexual desires and*

urges. It is a daily battle that we must fight if we are to please Him.),
and (3) look at all people the way Christ sees them *(Men should
look at women as their sisters in Christ, not as sex objects. Women
should look at men as brothers in Christ. If you are dating someone,
your focus should be on interacting with them based on the Word of
God and not on the will of your own selfish desires.)*

Q9: Who is a spiritual father? What are the characteristics of a good spiritual father? Why do I need one?

A9: In Psalm 128, the psalmist describes the importance of a
man on the impact of the family, church and country. It is the job
of the father to disciple and influence his family with a Christ-
Centered worldview. The father's role is to provide wisdom and
guidance about life, which certainly includes the selection process
of a mate.

If a man or a woman does not have a father who is alive or who is a
Christian then ideally the church should act as the father and guide
him/her in spiritual matters. And marriage is definitely a spiritual
matter. The community of believers (the church) and its leaders
should act as fathers for singles (1 Cor. 4:14-15; 1 Thess. 2:11-12).

A good spiritual father should first, be a fully devoted follower of
Jesus Christ (Matt. 22:37-40 and Matt. 28:19-20). He should
also make wise and spiritual decisions based on the Word of God
(1 Cor. 2:15). Finally, he should be a good role model in speech,

in life, in love, and in faith (1 Tim. 4:12).

Here are three final things to remember. First, it's ok to have a mentor couple or spiritual "parents". Clearly, a couple can provide great insight for you on your journey of life and spiritual growth. Second, if you can't find good candidates in your church ask God to show you other options. It is God's desire that single men and women have this covering so He'll provide what you need. You will be surprised how He allows other family members or father figures to step forward. Lastly, a woman should try her best to ensure there are no unhealthy emotions between her and the man she chooses as a spiritual father. If the two of you have anything other than a familial type of relationship (brother/sister, father/daughter, uncle/niece, etc.) just move on! Avoid the drama!

Q10: If women should not initiate relationships with men why was it acceptable for Ruth to initiate with Boaz (Ruth 3:6-9)?

A10: Ruth's situation was a unique one. To understand her action, you must first understand her cultural context. Ruth was a widow and according to the law, during that time, the responsibility of providing for widows was extended to the next of kin—usually a brother. If there was no brother to raise the children and provide for the widow, the responsibility of provision was passed to the next closest relative. The law also required the initiative of the widow in the seeking marriage since widows were not obligated to remarry. Although Boaz was not Ruth's closest relative, he

132

was who Naomi, her mother-in-law, recommended. So in this case, Ruth was being obedient to her covering (Naomi) and the law. Sometimes, women use this story to justify their initiation in relationships. However, a closer look at the context reveals the true meaning of Ruth's actions.

Q11: What do I do if I'm already in a relationship but I now see that we need to step back and re-evaluate it or maybe even end it?

A11: If the person you're in a relationship with is a non-Christian (unbeliever), you should graciously, yet firmly, end the relationship. Just let the person know (without guilt, judgment or ultimatum) that the relationship (<u>not the person</u>) prevents you from prioritizing your faith. Remember, we should never be bound to unbelievers (2 Cor. 6:14).

On the other hand, if you realize there are more delicate issues at hand, you should take a few days to seek God through prayer. Allow your mind, heart and emotions to all get on the same page so you can think as objectively as possible. Relationship issues often don't have cut and dry solutions and you want to make sure you handle the situation with care. You should also consult your spiritual father or mentor for wisdom on how to proceed.

You may decide one of two things: first, you may decide to end the relationship for a number of reasons. If this is the case, make sure you clearly communicate with the other person, and let them know why you are ending the relationship. It's not wise to get into specifics because it may tempt the other person to change or conform to your request just to stay in the relationship. For example, it's safe to let him/her know that you believe the relationship is unhealthy because you believe the relationship is spiritually, emotionally or physically unhealthy.

Second, you may decide to stay in the relationship with a mutual agreement to take action to make the relationship healthier (pursue counseling, meet with a mentor or couple, etc.). In this case, after seeking God in prayer and talking with your spiritual advisors, share your concerns with the person you're in a relationship with. Let him/her know your thoughts and your suggested resolutions. Be open to their thoughts and feelings and be willing to have authentic (maybe even painful) dialogue to reach an agreement without comprising your principles.

Most importantly, whenever you are ending a relationship or raising issues that need answers, remember to always take responsibility for your role in the demise or misdirection of the relationship. Whether you are a man or a woman, there is usually a boundary you didn't set clearly, a principle you didn't prioritize, or communication you didn't provide that could have contributed to the problems in the relationship. When it's all said and done, people should leave relationships with their heart and emotions in tact. Not that there won't be pain or hurt – but there should not be damage.

get focused

about the authors

Conway Z.C. Edwards

Dr. Conway Edwards is the Singles Ministry Director and Pastoral Assistant to Dr. Anthony T. Evans, the Senior Pastor at Oak Cliff Bible Fellowship (OCBF) in Dallas, Texas. He was previously the Director of Spiritual Formation at OCBF, a position he held for three years. Conway also served as a leadership fellow at Dallas Theological Seminary in the Center for Christian Leadership, under the leadership of Dr. Howard Hendricks.

Under his leadership, the Singles Ministry at Oak Cliff Bible Fellowship has grown in a year and a half from an average of 35 singles to over 700 in small groups and over 500 in their monthly singles gathering. The ministry has been marked by creativity, a commitment to excellence, volunteer involvement, and most importantly a genuine desire to live for God.

Conway received his Master of Theology, with an emphasis in Pastoral Leadership, from Dallas Theological Seminary. He received his Doctor of Strategic Leadership from Regent University in Virginia. Conway holds a Master of Business Administration with an emphasis in Human Resources. He teaches in the field of leadership and consults in leadership on a part-time basis for many churches and conferences across the United States and Jamaica. Some of the churches include: Grace Church of Glendora in Glendora,

136

California; Pinon Hills Community Church in Farmington, New Mexico; St. Luke Baptist Church, in Little Rock Arkansas; New Faith Church in Houston, Texas. Some of the conferences include: the Iron Sharpens Iron Leadership Conference in Dubuque, Iowa; The Urban Alternative's Church Development Conference, held in Dallas, Texas; the National Centre for Christian Leadership Mentoring Conferences in Jamaica.

Conway is the Executive Director for the US-based ministry Caribbean Choice for Christ, a ministry that seeks to train and develop leaders to impact their institutions and communities with the gospel of Jesus Christ. He is also the Founder and President of the Jamaica-based National Centre for Christian Leadership-Jamaica (NCCLJ). These nonprofit organizations specialize in leadership consulting and leadership development and seek to equip leaders with biblically based strategies for effective church, civic, and professional leadership. Conway's desire is to see God bring forth 52,000 male Christian leaders on the island of Jamaica who understand their calling and are impacting their communities with a Christ-centered worldview.

Jamaica is Conway's original home, and discipling men and developing leaders are Conway's passions. He firmly believes in and spends much of his time embracing the 2 Timothy 2:2 charge of mentoring and discipling other men.

Jada A. Edwards

Jada Edwards is the Process Analyst for the Dallas County Community College District (DCCCD) with over 55,000 enrolled students and eight educational campuses throughout Dallas County. Jada holds a Master of Business Administration with an emphasis in Organizational Strategy and has experience in improving organizations through process improvement and technological initiatives. She works in new business development, partner relations and marketing for Caribbean Choice for Christ, a U.S.-based nonprofit leadership organization, founded by her husband Conway. Their ministry focuses on developing and equipping Christian leaders all over the United States and Jamaica.

An experienced speaker, Bible teacher, and mentor, Jada has committed her life to equipping women of all ages, regardless of marital status, with practical, biblical truth to help them live more genuine lives. She has served in various directional capacities within the youth and singles ministries at Oak Cliff Bible Fellowship, a church with over 1,000 youth and 3,000 singles. Jada currently resides in Dallas, Texas, with her husband Conway.

For booking information, questions,
or comments contact us at:

What to do When Love's in View
P.O. Box 223743
Dallas, Texas 75222
email: whenlovesinview@yahoo.com

For more information about our
leadership development ministry
in the Caribbean please visit:

www.caribbeanchoice.org

Fri 13   1800-200

Sat - 14   - 9A - 120